ENDORSEMENTS

"In *Sola Deus*, Keith Giles addresses the most monumental post-religion question of our times: 'What is God?' Brilliant thinkers and philosophers through history have taken on this existential quest. But these are different times in the West. Traditional Christian Theism has lost its footing. An increasingly secular culture says, 'Who needs God?' We needed Keith Giles to write this book, and just in the nick of time. Keith masterfully explores the landscape of God after religion. Bump this book to the top of your reading list. You can thank me later."

JIM PALMER, Founder and Director of the
Center for Non-Religious Spirituality, Author of Inner Anarchy

"There are few things I love more than a lively theological conversation with a friend. In *Sola Deus*, Keith Giles invites us into one of those conversations. This is not a book of easy or safe answers, but rather a bold and engaging invitation to life's greatest questions. You will be challenged and you will be changed."

RANDAL RAUSER, author of *Progressive Christians Love Jesus Too*

"It has become common to reject the idea God is 'out there,' distant from us. But what might it mean for God to be here, with, and in us? In what sense might we be divine, as 'partakers of the divine nature,' to quote scripture? Keith Giles explores these questions in this readable book and offers nuanced answers. I recommend this to those willing to engage *huge* questions about our relation to God!"

THOMAS JAY OORD, author of *Open and Relational Theology*, and other books

"Keith Giles has done it again. I appreciate that he keeps contributing to the deconstruction conversation in deeper and wider ways. In *Sola Deus: What If God Is All Of Us?*, Keith stretches the boundaries of our theological and spiritual thinking even further where the philosophers, mystics, and scientists play. I will recommend this book to people who desire a deep dive into why they're deconstructing their beliefs and wonder where it may lead them."

DAVID HAYWARD, the Naked Pastor, author of *Flip It Like This!*

KEITH GILES

SOLA
DEUS

WHAT IF GOD IS
All of Us?

Copyright © 2023 by Keith Giles
First Edition

Cover Design by Rafael Polendo (polendo.net)
Interior Layout by Matthew J. Distefano

Scriptures taken from the Holy Bible, New International Version®, NIV®. Copyright © 1973, 1978, 1984, 2011 by Biblica, Inc.™ Used by permission of Zondervan. All rights reserved worldwide. www.zondervan.com The "NIV" and "New International Version" are trademarks registered in the United States Patent and Trademark Office by Biblica, Inc.™

ISBN 978-1-957007-67-0, Printed in the United States of America

Published by Quoir
Chico, California
www.quoir.com

TABLE OF CONTENTS

DEDICATION

THIS BOOK IS DEDICATED to my wife, Wendy, without whom this book would certainly not exist. You're my best friend, my dream come true and the love of my life. Thank you for everything you do.

SPECIAL THANKS

The author would like to thank Matthew J. Distefano for being the best co-publisher and podcast co-host a guy could ever dream of. Thanks also to my sons Dylan and David for always reminding me why creativity matters. Finally, thank you Joyce Anne Ferrell Giles, my Mom, for always being my biggest fan.

ALSO BY THE AUTHOR

"God shows up, again and again, to enter into relationship with humanity, and to show how far God is willing to go to bring humanity to Godself."

CORY DRIVER

FOREWORD

"I pray God to rid me of God."

MEISTER ECKHART

I remember sitting in a Zoom meeting with Keith Giles in December 2022 to talk about the marketing plan for my debut book, which would release in two short months with his publishing company, Quoir Publishing. I wish I could say I was equally excited and nervous, but, truthfully, I was probably eighty percent nerves at that point. You see, when you cement something very vulnerable in a book, you fear two things: being misunderstood, and being understood. It's quite the emotional conundrum.

Keith and I talked through all sorts of logistics for the marketing plan. At some point, he asked me if I was excited. "Uh...I think so," I replied, perhaps coyly. This sparked Keith's curiosity. "What do you mean?" Keith asked. "Well...I feel like I'm going to be the one to tell people there's no Santa Claus." I was serious. It wasn't a joke.

A somber look briefly flashed across Keith's face. "Yeah," he said. We lingered in the pause for just a moment and then moved on. But, for that moment, it felt like the same string had been plucked in both of our hearts at once. I could feel that note ring across the computer screen as we looked at one another through the camera. At that time, I didn't know that *Sola Deus* was about to flow out of Keith. Now that I've read it, I understand why I felt a kindred spirit with him in that meeting.

If you're already at all familiar with Keith Giles, you know that he shoots you straight. He's willing to tell the truth, even when he knows it will cost him. He's been a voice for many who are questioning their assumptions and beliefs, assuring people it's okay to ask the questions you aren't supposed to ask, and helping thousands to reimagine the Christian faith—not for the sake of reimagining alone, but for the love of truth itself. His love and admiration for Jesus is unquestionable. I can't think of anyone else who has written a seven-part book series with each book having the name "Jesus" in the title! Keith has taken seriously the role of student of Jesus, and we are all better for it.

However, I couldn't help but feel that, in addition to thought-provoking and paradigm-shifting ideas, there's a bit of a confessional happening in this book. While, in the past, you may have found Keith to be a comforting companion in your questioning, it's evident in this book that Keith has come to a threshold in his life—one that is beautiful and expansive, but also painful. He acknowledges several times that, while he's leading the reader into new depths, these frontiers might feel more frightening than before. This might be too much, and that's okay.

In these pages, Keith acts simultaneously as the purveyor of ideas—ideas that are possibly difficult but exciting, uncomfortable but intriguing, painful but liberating—and also as the compassionate friend who shows up when you're disoriented. He's both a maverick and a grounding presence. Personally, I've found that I don't want to explore revelatory ideas with anyone who is not both of those things, lest I go off a cliff for which I'm not prepared. Mavericks are fairly easy to find, often the product of personality traits. A deeply-rooted presence takes time and intention to cultivate within, and that is harder to come by.

Two things that cannot be questioned in Keith's writing are his integrity and his empathy. He tells the truth, and then sits with you in it. But I got the distinct feeling that, more than the fear of being misunderstood, Keith knows that what he's conveying in these pages may be understood completely, and that might be worse. The power of these ideas has the potential to create greater kinship, compassion, understanding, and intimacy among his readers. Or the opposite. That's the inherent risk of telling the truth. I, for one, am thankful Keith took the risk. I feel more understood and less alone. I hope you'll experience the same.

In this book, Keith lays it all out there. Where he is now, where he was wrong in the past, where he's still unsure. He's tender, yet direct. While I have wrestled with these ideas via lofty texts from theologians and philosophers who I deeply respect, Keith speaks plainly in his familiar style that is instantly relatable. For those of us who have had our illusions about God smashed multiple times, there's a timbre of surrender you'll recognize. A simultaneous grief for what's been lost, and a liberating release into the ecstasy of Mystery. There's a sober happiness to his tone.

Still, the smasher of illusions is not a role one typically revels in, even if you're worthy of such a role (which Keith is). This sensitivity to the pain of lost illusions is precisely what qualifies Keith to write this book. He understands what the journey will cost, but is also willing to walk it. He's the kind of friend that stays true to his journey, yet understands if you cannot come with him. He graciously offers an off-ramp at several points in the book, which I encourage you to take if you need to. Compassionate writers anticipate the feelings of their readers, and that is on display here.

But in the end, I see a man whose path has led to an expansive field. A journey supposedly leading to a fixed point suddenly opens up into infinite Mystery. A road that seemed walled-in turns out to have a panoramic view. This will require that you read not just with your head, but with your heart, body, and soul.

If you can muster the courage, in these pages, Keith will lead you to the edge of what, at first, appears to be nowhere—but turns out to be everywhere. If you can let these words lead you past the boundaries of what you think you know, past the ideas and illusions you have about God, you may just experience the ineffable, breathtaking, expansive Mystery of life itself, and come to the same confession as Keith:

Sola Deus.

HEATHER HAMILTON, bestselling author of
Returning to Eden: A Field Guide for the Spiritual Journey

"God is inside us, and inside God is everything. And so whoever loves God loves all that is."

JULIAN OF NORWICH

INTRODUCTION

When I wrote my previous book, *Sola Mysterium: Celebrating the Beautiful Uncertainty of Everything*, I expected some pushback from the usual sources, but not from within the small circle of authors and progressive thinkers who once endorsed my writings. I wasn't prepared for comments like, "It frankly sounds like a Rob Bell-ish eruption of post-modern inclusivity and relativism," and "I am concerned that this book will damage your reputation and credibility among the Christians you're trying to reach," and "If Sola *Mysterium* represents what you might consider an adequately reconstructed Christian faith, then this is simply not a faith I would encourage people to embrace," and, my favorite criticism, "You sound like Richard Rohr!"

So, when I received feedback like this, and warnings from people I respect saying, "As a friend, I would sincerely encourage you not to publish this book," it really gave me pause.

Still, I had to be honest. I had to admit that the ideas in *Sola Mysterium* really were an accurate representation of where I was at and what I believed about God in that moment. I couldn't pretend to think something else. I knew I had to say what I felt needed to be said, come hell or high water.

Once the book was published the responses were mostly very positive. I had a few people accuse me of going too far, or of leaving the faith, but by and large the feedback was mostly in the form of gratitude for having the courage to step out and say what I did. I have no regrets about any of that now.

Here and there I received private messages telling me that some of my peers who had objected to the book privately were now going out of their way to warn other people to steer clear of me because of the ideas I shared in *Sola Mysterium*. This was very disappointing. But at least one of those authors who disagreed with my ideas had the integrity to approach me privately and ask me to engage in a private email conversation where we could both try to understand where the other was coming from. I only wish all of those who disagreed with my ideas in that book had extended me the same grace.

Still, here I am sitting down a few months later to write yet another book about God that I know in advance will ruffle those same feathers and invite the same sort of attacks from those who once called me "brother" and "friend." Some might wonder why I would continue to write books that rock the boat and invite these sorts of criticism. I can assure you it's not because I have any love for controversy.

Truth be told, I really don't enjoy losing friends and being labelled a heretic or a false teacher. Sure, I joke about those titles and have fun with the notion that a heretic is anyone who disagrees with you—as if you alone are the standard for all truth in the universe and you couldn't possibly be wrong about anything. To be honest, when I get those messages accusing me of leading people astray or teaching false doctrine, it hurts. Especially when those messages come from people who previously supported me and endorsed my writings. That level of rejection is deeply painful and disturbing.

Yet, here I am again, writing another book about God and reality and faith from a perspective that I know beyond any doubt will push me even further outside the realm of acceptability for many.

So, why am I doing this? Why am I writing down my thoughts and perspectives about God if I know it will only call down more condemnation from those self-appointed gatekeepers of Christianity?

Because first of all, I can't help myself. I'm a writer. Writers write. So, when I learn something new or come across an idea that genuinely excited me, I must sit down to write about it. It's just who I am. It's how I process ideas.

Secondly, I write books like this one because of all the amazing encouragement I receive from readers who tell me my books have set them free, or given them peace, or helped them to make sense of things that were previously incomprehensible. Those messages are so precious to me I actually save them in a folder on my computer just so I can remind myself why I do this, and why books like this one matter so much to people who are enchanted by the never-ending mystery of God.

So, that's why I'm sitting here, now, writing another book. Because I have even more ideas to share, and because I know that some of these chapters here might contain the catalyst for an extraordinary process of transformation for readers like yourself.

That's my hope, at least; to inspire and to provoke a sense of renewed awe and wonder into your everyday routine.

In the previous book, I suggested that there was more of Christ to know than any of us could ever know in this lifetime.

In this book, I want to explore the mysterious connection between God and Humanity—the Spirit and the Flesh—and perhaps even shift your paradigm of the Divine in directions you have possibly never even considered before.

These are ideas that have only recently taken shape in my own heart and mind. They are ideas that have set me free from old ways of thinking about God, and myself. They are ideas that, I believe, are more consistent with the wisdom I see in the red letters of Jesus's teaching, and the epistles of the Apostle Paul, as well as among the writings of the mystics and philosophers like Socrates, Teresa of Avila, Buddha, Thoreau, Valentinus and Khalil Gibran, to name a few.

Simply put, the ideas in this book will challenge us to rethink our image of God; the nature of God, the character of God, the essence of God, and these thoughts will—and must—cause us to rethink our image of humankind, and of ourselves, as well.

Please understand, I am not attempting to define God, because no one can do that. I am not looking to understand God intellectually. That is impossible. But I do hope to shine a light on the ways that many of us have been taught to think about God and to expose the misunderstandings that may have been subconsciously imposed on our conception of God.

My hope is that, by identifying some of the ways we have misunderstood who and what God is, we might become even more aware of a God who defies our paradigms and transcends our false assumptions.

In the same way that Abraham needed to realize that God was not like the other gods who demanded child sacrifice, or that Jacob needed to understand that God was not confined to one Holy patch of ground but was with him wherever he went, or that Peter needed to see that God had never called anyone unclean, we, also, need to have a new revelation about who God is—and is not—so our connection with God can come into sharper focus and our understanding of our identity as God's image bearers—the *imago Dei*—can be more fully realized.

We'll begin by exploring the idea that God's plan all along has always been for us to let go of our elementary understandings so we can move forward into a maturity that takes us beyond the doctrines of our faith.

Are you ready? I hope so. Your journey begins when you turn this page.

"The world is crowded with God. The real labor is to remember, to attend. In fact, to come awake. Still more, to remain awake."

C.S. LEWIS

Chapter 1

TALKING ABOUT GOD

From my earliest days as a small boy laying in my bed at night, talking to God like an imaginary friend, to the young man walking with God in the mountains of New Mexico at a college retreat, to the much older man sitting down to write a series of books about the character, nature and mystery of the Divine, I've spent most of my life thinking about God.

In terms of my own experience, I would have to say that I find it much easier to think about God than to talk about God. Part of the reason for that, I believe, is that our language systems are wholly inadequate to the task.

For example, I have tried lately to avoid using gender pronouns whenever I talk about God, but that has proven to be much more difficult than I first imagined. That's because our language requires us to use "He" or "She" or "It" to qualify the subject of any sentence, and once you've started to identify your subject as "God," you will eventually find yourself needing to use a pronoun to continue your thought, and if you've decided not to use "He" or "She" or "It" you're not left with many options. This creates a very clunky sentence. You may start to notice the times in this book that I have borrowed the term "Godself" rather than say "Himself" or "Herself" in reference to God.

The reason I try to avoid those pronouns is to avoid suggesting, even subtly, that God is a male or a female, or even a discrete being like us who floats around somewhere up there or out there. Our language shapes our ideas in ways we are often not consciously aware of. So, the more I can avoid those anthropomorphic terminologies, the better chance I have of communicating more accurate ideas about God to help shape our imaginations as we try to discuss the nature and character of God.

It isn't easy. Even in my own thoughts I tend to fall back into those old habits of using gendered pronouns for God. Old habits can be hard to break. That's why I say that it's easier to think about God than it is to talk about God. Because to talk about God—or to write a book about God—we have to use language, and our language wasn't designed to talk about a concept or a being as challenging as God.

But we can think about God without reverting to language. We can experience the presence of God without needing to narrate everything to ourselves, or to others. The experience of God is something that transcends language and goes straight into our consciousness.

Perhaps this is because, when we think about God, our consciousness is in direct connection with the consciousness of God.

If God is the ultimate consciousness, then when our consciousness resonates with the frequency of God's consciousness, there is no need for words or language, and to introduce language into the process greatly diminishes and dilutes the experience.

This is why we don't spend as much time talking about love as we do giving and sharing and experiencing love. Love is something we all know and understand, but when it comes to communicating exactly what love is like, or how it makes us feel, or even what it really is, our words fall woefully short.

Not that this prevents us from trying. Just think of how many poems, songs and stories have been written to capture the feeling or essence of love. Hundreds of thousands of sonnets, love songs and screenplays have been penned over the millennia to celebrate the beauty, intimacy and intricate drama inspired by love in all of its myriad forms.

A love song can strike that deepest chord within our souls that transports us to a place and time where that emotional resonance was first encountered. A poem can provoke a sense of yearning and longing within us that makes us hunger for the touch of our beloved. A movie can immerse us in the expressions of love shared between two people and remind us of our own experiences of love.

But, as beautiful and as compelling as those poems, songs, films and stories are, they are no substitute for the real thing. Feeling loved and loving another person is far and away more necessary and vital to us than listening to songs about love, or reading about it in a poetry book, or watching actors play their parts in a romantic film.

Love is meant to be experienced. Love is meant to be expressed to another person. Love is a verb. So, talking about love, and singing about love may come naturally to us, but it's the actual experience of loving and being loved that really makes the difference.

So, if we keep in mind that God is love, then perhaps all of this theological rambling begins to fade into the background. Maybe it's as fruitless to write about God as it is to confine love to a rhyming verse of poetry. And maybe we are as helpless to stop talking about God as we are from not singing about love. Part of our human experience is to express our feelings in words, or song, or in our art. That's not something we can necessarily control. Nor should we. But, if our world were inundated with songs and books and poems and films about love but none of us had any actual experience of love, how dark and empty that world would be. And if our world is consumed with theological arguments and religious conflicts over who has the right ideas of God, but none of us actually ever experienced the breathtaking presence or exquisite tenderness of God for ourselves, how much darker could our world become?

This is the tension: Between thinking and talking about a being of love so transcendent and glorious, and experiencing the ineffable presence of God's being within ourselves in ways that words cannot ever express.

So, here I am writing a book about God and adding more words to the ever-increasing number of pages being published around the globe about who God is and what God is like. But do I spend time in the silence? Do I take walks in the afternoon to listen to God's voice? Do I look for God's face in the people around me? Am I aware of God's inescapable loving presence permeating my soul and filling everyone and everything around me? These things are more important than writing about God or talking about God.

My question to you, my dear reader, is do you spend time doing these things? I think that's what really matters. At the end of the day, when all of the books have been written, and all of the songs have been sung, what really matters is simply this: Have you experienced the love of God? Do you know that you are treasured beyond imagination? Are you aware of how precious and unique you are to the One who made you in the same image of love that breathed life itself into being?

Remember, as wonderful as it is to learn about God and to meditate on Christ, we must take care not to allow these mental exercises to take the place of actually becoming intimate with God. This is what really counts. No book can duplicate that knowing within you. No song can unlock that awareness. It's already whispering deep within you. Even now. It's right here. In the silence. In every beat of your heart. Within every inhalation of oxygen into your lungs.

You are loved.

You are treasured.

You are adored.

Whatever it takes, my friend. I recommend you find that voice. Whatever stands in the way of that awareness, remove it now. Cancel that appointment. Reschedule that meeting. Find yourself deep within the heart of the One who is found in you.

In this book we're going to talk about God and think about God a lot. But I hope that all of this thinking and talking doesn't eclipse your direct personal connection with the Divine. If anything, your awareness of your connection with God will help us process these ideas together in a much greater way than if you're simply reading and thinking without actually experiencing God's presence along the way.

Are you ready to begin? Let's go.

"At no point in the evolutionary history of this planet has any organism at any point ever seen reality as it is."

DR. DON HOFFMAN, COGNITIVE SCIENTIST

Chapter 2
THE METANOIA REALITY

IF YOU'VE SPENT ANY time rethinking your faith and questioning the religious beliefs you were handed when you were younger, you'll understand how painful and disorienting it can be.

Not only do you have to endure the pain of losing close friends and even family members who cannot accept your shift in beliefs, you may also have to suffer the condemnation from pastors as they call you a heretic, or an apostate for daring to challenge the status quo.

Yet, in spite of these things, the seeds of what some have called deconstruction are sown by Jesus in the very first sermon he preached almost two thousand years ago when he said, "Repent!" or, literally in the Greek, "Metanoia!" which simply means to think differently or change your mind.

So, asking questions, challenging religious assumptions and changing your mind about theology is something Jesus seems to not only value, but he also even seems to suggest that, without these things, we cannot possibly receive the message he has for us.

For the last few decades that's exactly what I've found myself doing over and over again—changing my mind and thinking differently about everything I once believed. I've paid the price for exposing toxic theology and lost both family and friends along the way. But, as you may know, once you've seen something, you can't unsee it, and once you know something, you can't unknow it.

Even our ways of approaching the concept of "knowing" might need to be reconsidered once we start to examine our beliefs and our assumptions about God.

What if it's not about having all the answers? What if it's more about moving forward into the unknown, propelled by the continual series of questions we encounter as we move deeper into the endless depths of God.

This approach keeps us in a perpetual state of awe and wonder. It requires us to maintain a continuous attitude of metanoia—rethinking our assumptions—about everything, all of the time.

Doing this also requires us to develop a new set of muscles that many of us have never been taught how to use in our everyday lives. The practice of listening, of waiting in the silence, of looking at the world with new eyes and from different perspectives, doesn't come naturally to most of us. In fact, most of those things were highly discouraged by our prior religious mentors and teachers. They warned us to avoid meditation and cautioned us not to trust our own ability to hear God's voice. Instead, they told us it was safer to just set all of that aside and trust in their ability to hear God's voice for us. Many of us have spent way too many years of our lives trusting those other people's ability to listen to God. Now that we've realized that was a mistake, we have to begin learning to trust ourselves and our own capacity for connecting directly with God without asking anyone else for assistance, or permission.

Simply put, deconstruction is essential to spiritual growth and maturity. But it's not always an easy road, and many of us have the scars to prove it.

After wrestling with my faith and questioning the answers I was given for so many years now, I eventually came across this passage in the book of Hebrews that not only tells us to rethink our theology, but that growing in our faith simply can't be accomplished without letting go of those foundational doctrines of Christianity.

Seriously. Here's the verse from Hebrews chapter 6, verses 1 to 3:

"Therefore, *let us move beyond the elementary teachings about Christ* and *be taken forward to maturity, not laying again the foundation of repentance* from acts that lead to death *[sin]*, and of *faith in God, instruction about cleansing rites, the laying on of hands, the resurrection of the dead, and eternal judgment.* And God permitting, we will do so."

Do you see what this is saying? The author of Hebrews tells us that, in order to "be taken forward to maturity" we have to "move beyond the elementary teachings of Christ" which include things like Sin, Faith in God, Religious Traditions, Prayer, the Resurrection, and Eternal Judgment.

Not only do most Christians today totally ignore this verse—or are completely ignorant of the very existence of such a verse in their Bible—they spend almost their entire Christian life focusing entirely on those specific things.

So, what is holding us back from moving towards maturity? It's exactly these elementary doctrines that have become the dominant points of contention within Christianity as we know it. The incessant arguments about the unforgivable sin, or the bodily resurrection, or the continual confession and repentance rituals that take place every Sunday in churches across the globe, or the debates over which view of Hell is true and which ones are heresy; all of these only keep us running in circles around the spiritual mulberry bush rather than looking up from our Bibles long enough to notice that there's an entire universe of wonder, awe and mystery that we've yet begun to explore.

As some of us have experienced first-hand, many of these doctrines create very real emotional and psychological trauma that may take us years to work through and find healing from. And the focus on who is right and who is wrong creates division and separation in the form of religious denominations, but also—sadly—in the form of lost friendships and even divisions between family members.

So, if we seek to move beyond these elementary teachings and be taken forward into maturity, then letting go of our obsession with religious arguments is extremely crucial. It means we need to stop obsessing over our sins, or worrying about who has the right faith in God, or about religious purity, or prayer, or arguments about the resurrection or about who's going to hell or heaven.

All of that is what keeps us from moving forward into maturity. Those are the elementary level subjects that, by now, we should have already understood and processed. I think this is why our deconstruction journey is so important: because once we've questioned and reconsidered all of those introductory theological concepts, we are finally ready for the next level of our spiritual development.

In fact, if you have not already questioned and processed and reconsidered your initial theological indoctrination, I'm not sure you're truly prepared for what's next.

This is why Jesus kicked off his first sermon with such a radical idea: Think different! Because until you first question the framework of your theological universe, you're not ready for the radical concepts of God's Kingdom.

The metaphor Jesus used to describe this phenomenon was to compare old wineskins to new ones:

> "And no one pours new wine into old wineskins. Otherwise, the wine will burst the skins, and both the wine and the wineskins will be ruined. No, they pour new wine into new wineskins." [Mark 2:22]

So, first, we have to endure this process of transformation from within. We have to enter the spiritual cocoon, experience the process of transformation from the inside out, and then, once we've been made new, we can finally receive that new wine that God wants to pour inside of us.

That's why the deconstruction process is so essential to our spiritual growth process. Without it, we can't even begin to fully receive everything that God wants to do in and through us.

This realization should give us hope, by the way. It should help us to see that enduring that painful season of doubt and uncertainty was all part of God's intention and purpose for us from the very beginning. Now that we've come out the other side, we're new creatures who are ready to think differently; we are like new wineskins that are ready to receive the new wine and to perceive a new reality.

This process isn't a one-time event. It's something we must endure over and over again as we continually rethink our assumptions and challenge our own status quo.

A few years ago, as I was studying the history of the early Christian church I came across a phrase that many of them used as a sort of rallying cry: *Conversatio Morem!* It turns out there are two ways to translate this term. One of them is "Death to the Status Quo!" which might make for a great tattoo if I were to ever want one. But the other way of translating this term is "Constant Conversion!" which, if I'm honest, is not only a lot cooler, it's even harder to live out. Because rather than just shout the words, "Death to the Status Quo!", what we really need to do is to realize that this process of ongoing metanoia requires us to adopt an ongoing commitment to defy our own status quo. That constant conversion concept is what helps us to hold loosely to our beliefs and to embrace uncertainty at all times.

So, if we're going to do this then all of those elementary concepts that we tend to cling to must be released. Everything that holds us back must be abandoned. Every hindrance in our journey towards maturity must be thrown off.

Here, we enter the next phase of our spiritual path. As Jesus instructed his disciples when he sent them out into the unknown, "Take nothing with you for the journey—no staff, no bag, no bread, no money, no extra clothing" so, we, too, must be willing to leave everything behind in order to walk the path that opens before us. The path that leads over the distant horizon ahead.

The path that leads to a place we have never been, or seen, or even imagined before.

Here, at the crossroads, we must drop everything we cling to; our assumptions, our convictions, and our certainty. Especially our certainty.

The Truth, as many have observed, lies just beyond our comfort zone. With every step we take—from this point forward—our journey takes us deeper into the metanoia reality. Everything must change. Every idea must be challenged. Every assumption must be transformed. That means our ideas and our beliefs, our hearts and our minds.

There's a great line from a film called Mary Magdalene where Peter and Mary are expressing very different perspectives about what to do now that Jesus has been crucified, resurrected, and taken up into heaven. Peter says that they all need to wait for Jesus to return because he had promised to bring the Kingdom and it hadn't happened yet. Mary turns to Peter and says, "No, the world will only change if we change." And that's what we need to realize too, my friends. The change we seek starts within. The transformation of the world begins within you, and within me, and within every single one of us.

The way Christ changes the world is by changing us from the inside out. So, our focus should be on embracing that change and being constantly open to that transformation process.

When we are transformed, the world is too. When we let go of those elementary teachings and set our faces towards the great unknown before us, we are standing at the beginning of what comes next.

So, are you ready to let go of those rudimentary beliefs you were indoctrinated with? Are you prepared to lay aside your need to be right about the resurrection, or sin, or eternal judgment?

If so, this book may be a gift to you. If not, you may wish you had never opened the cover or started reading.

Here is where we begin to leave behind those elementary things, my friend.

"I would rather live in a world where my life is surrounded by mystery than live in a world so small that my mind could comprehend it."

HENRY EMERSON FOSDICK

Chapter 3

RETHINKING GOD

I want you to imagine something. What if there was a child, a baby girl, and she's born in a remote part of the world that is cut off from modern society.

She doesn't speak English. She can't read. She has never experienced electricity or running water. She doesn't know what indoor plumbing is and has never purchased anything from another person using money.

Her world is primitive. Her days are filled with gathering food for her tribe, swimming with her friends in the nearby river, and listening to her grandmother tell stories about their ancestors around the fire circle every evening under the stars that twinkle and shine above her in the night sky.

Now, let me ask you something. *Can this little girl know God? Can she hear God's voice? Can she experience a profound connection with the Divine?*

If you say no, then why not? Does she need someone to come and teach her religious doctrine first? Does she require a temple to channel God's presence? Must she learn to read first so God can speak to her through the Bible? Does she have to wait for a priest to arrive, or a missionary who can lay out the mechanics of spirituality for her?

I don't know about you, but I have come to the place in my life where I simply cannot accept the idea that what this little girl needs is theology, or a book, or a temple, or a priest, or anything else in order to experience the presence of God.

Why? Because God has never required any of those things to make Godself known. All of creation pulsates with the presence of the Divine. Every bird's song, every ripe fruit, every drop of rain, every night sky flung wide with stars is God's voice surrounding, penetrating, permeating every pore of our being.

Temples are not necessary for encountering God's presence. Priests are of little use for hearing the voice of God. Holy Books are a poor substitute for the experience of the Divine within your own heart and soul.

This little girl—and millions like her around the world—require none of these things to know God, or to experience God, or to hear the voice of God.

All this little girl needs to do is to look up at the sky, breathe deep the air, lie still beneath the trees, float peacefully on the water, sleep soundly under the stars, or simply close her eyes and feel the eternal loving presence of the Divine in her own heart.

That's all you need to do, too.

You don't need any pastor, or church, or Bible to know God's presence. You require no blessing, no baptism and no religious indoctrination to experience the Divine. You need nothing except to be still and know that God is everywhere, all around you, and within you.

In fact, as we've already seen, those very things that others have convinced us we need in order to know God—the pastor, the Bible, the church, right theology—may very well be the things that prevent us from knowing God or experiencing God.

So, whatever you do, don't allow anyone else to mediate your connection with God. God's spirit has been poured out on all flesh: young and old, men and women, rich and poor, gay and straight.

True Reality

In the Hindu faith, the concept of ultimate reality or the essence of the universe is something called *Satchitananda* which is a Sanskrit term that refers to the three attributes of the ultimate reality: Existence (Sat), Consciousness (Chit), and Bliss (Ananda).

According to Hindu philosophy, the universe is created from and sustained by this ultimate reality, and the ultimate goal of human life is to realize this reality and attain liberation (moksha). This concept of Satchitananda represents the fundamental nature of the universe and of the individual self (Atman).

Surprisingly, some Christian philosophers and theologians like David Bentley Hart interpret this same idea as "being, consciousness, and bliss" based on an understanding that the ultimate reality is not an abstract principle or substance, but the triune God of the Christian faith who is the source of all being, consciousness, and happiness. As he puts it:

> "Many Christians in India, moreover—like the Benedictine monk Henri le Saux (1910—1973)...the author of the great Trinitarian hymn Vande Satchidananda —have used these ancient Sanskrit words to describe their own understandings of God. And one finds analogous descriptions of the divine in all of the major theistic traditions. The great Sufi thinker Ibn Arabi (1165—1240), for instance, plays upon the common etymological root of the words wujud (being), wijdan (consciousness), and wajd (bliss) in order to describe the mystical knowledge of God as absolute Reality."[1]

Theologians like Hart believe that the triune God is the ground of all reality and that all things find their existence, meaning, and purpose in the Divine Being.

By announcing the inauguration of a New Covenant, Jesus proclaimed that the promise made in the Old Covenant scriptures was being fulfilled.

> *"This is the [new] covenant I will make...*, declares the LORD.
> *I will put My law in their minds and inscribe it on their hearts.*
> And I will be their God, and they will be My people. *No longer*

will each man teach his neighbor or his brother, saying, 'Know the LORD,' because they will all know Me, from the least of them to the greatest, declares the LORD. For I will forgive their iniquities and will remember their sins no more." [Jeremiah 31:33-34; Hebrews 8:10-11]

This promise—that everyone would know God directly, intimately and personally without the need for anyone else to mediate the experience—was now possible in ways people had not previously imagined. So, there is an intentional shift taking place.

In the same way that this little girl I described above who lives in a faraway land and doesn't read or speak English can still know and experience God's ineffable presence, you, and I, and everyone else alive on this planet, can also know and experience God.

God is not distant. God is not hiding away. God is as close to you as your very own heartbeat. As near as your very own breath.

The good news is that the entire world has been reconciled to God. So, now is the time to draw near. Now is the time to see for ourselves who God is and what God is like. There is absolutely nothing in your way. So, come. Be still. Breathe deep. God is all around you.

But, you may ask, "If God is a mystery, how can we understand God?" That's a very good question. In fact, sometimes our preconceptions about God may also keep us from better understanding how to relate to the Divine.

For example, many of us who were raised in the Evangelical Christian church have been conditioned to think of God as "up there" or "out there somewhere." As if we are down here on earth and God is up there above us in Heaven, wherever that may be.

This conception of God is based on an underlying assumption of separation between the Human and the Divine. God is God and we are not. God is up there and we are down here. God is Spirit and we are flesh. The division is inherent in almost every song we sing, or sermon we hear, or conversation we have.

But what if we're wrong about that? What if God is not "up there" or "out there" but "in here" with us? Some of us are already becoming convinced of this reality. We're starting to realize that our religious indoctrination included a built-in assumption of division and separation that not only isn't real, it's also not something ever taught by Jesus or the Apostle Paul.

So, who convinced us to think of God this way and to embrace this artificial concept of separation? Most likely it was the people who wanted to keep us coming back every week for another dose of momentary connection with the Divine. As if God could only meet us in the worship service, or in the pastor's sermon, or in the deacon's prayer, or on our knees at the altar call.

Once we start to realize that God has promised never to leave us nor forsake us, and that nothing in heaven or on earth could ever separate us from the love of God—a love which is higher, and wider, and longer and deeper than anyone could ever imagine—and that one of the names given to Jesus was "Emmanuel" which literally means "God with us", and that Jesus promised that he and the Father would make their home in every one of us, and abide in us as we abide in them...well, all of that other nonsense about separation and division starts to sound like a really bad sales pitch.

Now, as we've begun to accept the fact that we don't need to jump through any hoops to get something we already have, we finally realize that we don't need to strive for God's presence because God has made a home in each of us. We don't need to beg for God's attention because God is always present with us. We never have to beg God for forgiveness because the World has already been reconciled to God. We no longer have to confess our sins because we know that God keeps no record of wrongs.

So, when we let go of those false teachings about division and separation from God, we can start to experience the reality of God's presence.

But, what does that really mean? How can we make this shift from thinking about God as the One who is separated from us and start experiencing God as the One who fills everything in every way?

21

That's partly what this book is about. I hope to help us make that subtle, and yet profound, shift away from the God who is "high and lifted up" towards the God who is "the One in whom we all live, and move, and have our being."

Because one of those ways of thinking about God is reality, and the other is a carefully crafted illusion that religious leaders have created to keep us under their control.

The God who is too Holy to look upon our sin is not the God revealed by Jesus. The God who is out there and up there is not the God who actually permeates every molecule and atom in the Universe.

To know and experience God for who God is, we have to make this crucial break from the make-believe God who is the giant old man in the sky with the white beard who sits on a throne surrounded by hordes of angels. Because the real God doesn't sit on a throne in the heavens. The God of reality doesn't look like that or operate that way. The actual God we encounter is not separated from us by space, or time, or location, or position.

God is with us. God has drawn near. God desires to endow us with the exquisite blessing of God's own eternal presence. This is the God who is truly alive at this very moment. This is the God we are dancing with. This is the God we are drawn to like a moth to the flame.

Our access to this God is not limited in any way. So, when we talk to God we are not inviting God to come near, because God is already pulsing through your veins. When we ask God to move, we're not addressing a God who is in the heavens but a God who lives and breathes in this very moment with us. When we wonder why God doesn't do something, God wonders why we're still talking to a God up there who is far away rather than shifting to move in concert with the God who dwells within us.

The almost unbelievable truth is this: We are the ones in whom God lives, moves and has being. The only God we can see is the one we find reflected back to us in the mirror, or across the room in the faces of others who are made in the very same image of God as we are. Christ has no body now but yours and mine.

The problem with many of us—even those of us who have reimagined our faith—is that we still sometimes flip back and forth between these two concepts of God. We say we know that God is not far away, but then we act as if God doesn't know what's happening in our world. We say we know that nothing will ever separate us from God but then we pray and ask God to show up. We affirm that God is the One in whom we live and move and have our being, but then we wonder where God is in our time of need.

What I'm suggesting is that we make up our minds now, once and for all, that the only God there is is the God who is eternally present within all of us. There is no other God. Our words and actions and thoughts must shift along with this realization of God's permanent connection to all humanity.

Let's take some time to explore this concept of the illusion of separation from God in the next chapter.

"In that day you will realize that I am in the Father, and the Father is in me, and I am in you."

JESUS

Chapter 4
GOD IS ONE

ONE OF THE MOST challenging things about being an author is that once you write something down in your book, it becomes set in stone on some level.

This makes it especially difficult when you write about theological concepts because, at least in my experience, our ideas and beliefs can shift over time and then you end up having to correct yourself in later books.

For example, a few years ago, in my book *Jesus Undefeated*, I wrote a chapter regarding the concept of being in Christ. At the time, my view was that Christians—and only Christians—were in Christ because they had made a conscious decision to follow the teachings of Jesus in their daily lives. My point was that, while there were some verses that suggested that we were all in Christ, there were others that suggested an "if/then" scenario where only those who invited Christ into their lives could truly be "in Christ" and experience the life of Christ within. I even had what I thought was a great analogy of how an empty plastic water bottle could be submerged into the heart of the ocean and, therefore, it could be said that the bottle was "in the ocean," but as long as the cap remained on the bottle, the ocean was not "in the bottle." Which, while clever, didn't allow for the fact that, according to what Jesus and the Apostle Paul said, there is no possible way for a Christ-less vacuum to exist in the universe.

We'll talk more about all of that soon enough.

So, anyway, as my views on this subject have evolved over time, this has created some confusion for many of those who may read my previous books in a different order than how I wrote them. To those who have been perplexed by this ongoing process of progressive revelation in my books, I offer my sincerest apologies. There's not much I can do about this other than to go back and revise certain chapters to reflect my current views. But that in itself becomes an endlessly fruitless endeavor. My views about so many things have changed—and continue to change—so often that to attempt those ongoing revisions would occupy more of my time than simply writing a new book to reflect my current positions as they evolve.

That's sort of where I find myself now. I'm writing a book that, for some readers, may seem out of character or out of alignment with something I've written previously. For the most part, this can't be helped. All I can do is to say, this is where I am now; this is what I believe today, and as I continue to grow and think and wrestle with things, more changes are probably coming after the ink is dry on this book, or in the next one.

Having said all of that, let me try to catch everyone up to where I am on this question of "Is Christ in everyone?" or "Are we all in Christ?" because that will help us all to start from a common reference point.

As I said, my view on this question used to be that being "in Christ" or having "Christ in you" was conditional. But soon after publishing *Jesus Undefeated*, I came to a startling realization: *I was wrong*.

My realization shifted largely because of the ongoing conversations I was having with my then-co-host of the *Heretic Happy Hour Podcast*, Jamal Jivanjee. He and I would endlessly disagree on this question and anyone who listens to the first two years of that show will no doubt remember that he and I almost always ended up going around and around on this topic.

So, I'm grateful to Jamal for not allowing the cement to dry for me on this, and for always pushing back whenever he could. I'm also grateful to my friend Chuck McKnight who finally helped me to see something I had overlooked during that entire back-and-forth conversation on this question which was found in the final verse of chapter 1 of Ephesians which says that we are all filled with "the fullness of Christ who fills everything in every way."

That's what made me stop and reconsider everything I had believed up to that point. How could I argue that Christ was only in some of us when there were verses like this one that affirmed the notion that Christ "fills everything in every way"? It left me no wiggle room whatsoever to imagine a way in which someone might *not* be filled with Christ when the verse said that Christ filled *everything* in every way.

So, that made me go back and reevaluate my prior assumptions of the conditionality of being filled with Christ or being in Christ. Suddenly, all of those other verses that I once held at arm's length began to take on greater significance than I had previously believed. Which is why in my next book, *Jesus Unforsaken*, I revised my statements about all of this in terms of what I had learned in the interim.

To be honest, I was genuinely excited about this newfound realization of "Christ in all" and what it could really mean. I began to meditate on the idea that Christ was in everyone and that everyone was in Christ. It really underscored the notion of Universal Reconciliation [or *Apokatastasis*] which I had already embraced, and it forced me to reconsider what it means to be saved, and what it means to relate to other human beings—not as "Christians" or "Non-Christians" anymore but simply as people who, like me, are made in the image of God and dearly beloved of God.

Still, there were even more layers to this theological onion than I could possibly have imagined. Eventually, the more I followed this rabbit trail of "Oneness with Christ" the more I began to realize that my assumptions about God needed to shift, and my ideas about humanity as well.

This is where things start to get scary for some people. I'll try to be as gentle as possible, but the implications of this radical oneness may take some unexpected turns. I hope you'll stick with me.

First, let's establish the notion that everyone really is one with Christ and that Christ really is one with everything, and everyone. For me, that initial paradigm shift was accomplished by reexamining scripture verses where Jesus affirms this idea, and where the Apostle Paul spells it out in no uncertain terms.

I've already shared the verse in Ephesians above where Paul affirms that we are all "filled with the fullness of [Christ] who fills everything in every way." But, there's more where that came from.

Jesus suggests this radical oneness in two places. First, when he says, *"In that day you will realize that **I am in my Father, and you are in me, and I am in you.**"* [John 14:20; emphasis mine]

So, let's think about that for a moment. Jesus says that, eventually, you and I will come to a place where we are ready to consider the possibility that: A) Jesus is in the Father, B) We are in Jesus and C) Jesus is in us.

That's the first step. We have to stop and think about what it would mean to fully accept the notion that Jesus is in the Father, and that we are in Jesus, and that Jesus is in us. This is simply about our Oneness with God and with one another. Once we reach the point where we can grasp that idea, there comes a flood of additional considerations to ponder. But let's not jump to that just yet. Let's look at a few more passages first and then we'll circle back around to this, okay?

Jesus also offers up a prayer for us in the Gospel of John that reveals his hopes for us in the future; hopes that one day you and I might realize something quite marvelous, as he prays the following in conversation with the Father concerning all of us:

> "[I pray] that *they all may be one, just as you, Father, are in me, and I am in you, that they also may be in us*, so that the world may believe that you have sent me. The glory that you have given me I have given to them, *that they may be one even as we are one; I in them, and you in me, that they may become perfectly one...*" [John 17:21-23; emphasis mine]

This is quite a startling prayer, isn't it? First, Jesus prays that we "may all be one" even as the Father is in Jesus, and Jesus is in the Father. What does that mean? Think about it for a second. Try to imagine in what ways the Father is in Jesus, and to what degree Jesus is in the Father. Now, that same level of oneness is what Jesus wants all of us to experience with each other! This is not suggesting that we should merely be friends, or that we should all get along, or that we should play nice together. No, this is saying that we should be One in the exact same way that Jesus and the Father are One, which is quite frankly a mind-boggling idea.

Just look at that final sentence: *"that they may be one even as we are one; I in them and you in me, that they may become **perfectly one.**"* [emphasis mine]

Close your eyes for a second. Take a deep breath. Try to imagine being one with everyone in the same way that Jesus is one with the Father. I know, it's not easy, and it may even—at least at this moment—seem impossible. But, perhaps that's why Jesus qualified his earlier statement by suggesting that this is something that we might one day realize some time in the future; because it's a bit too much to fully accept all at once.

Just for fun, I tried to draw this concept out on a napkin in an attempt to visually understand what's being said here.

First, let's take what Jesus says in John 14: 20 and try to sketch it out:

This first sketch helps us understand what is being said, but if we think about it, the drawing doesn't represent reality because God doesn't fit inside any box. So, maybe we should draw it like this:

31

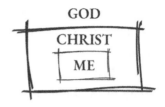

This is a little better now that we've taken God out of the box, but it's still not entirely accurate, is it? I mean, if Christ fills everything in every way, then Christ shouldn't be confined to a box either.

So, let's try this again:

That's a little better. God and Christ are no longer confined to boxes, but if I am in Christ and if Christ is in me, then there shouldn't be any separation between me and God, or between me and Christ. So, let's try this one more time:

GOD
CHRIST
ME

Okay, now we're getting there, but, once again, what Jesus is saying is that we are in Christ and Christ is in us, and we are all in one another, so maybe it should look something more like this:

GODCHRISTME

Or, better yet, how about this:

G<u>C</u>O<u>H</u>D<u>R</u>M<u>I</u>EST

That's probably more accurate, but it's also quite confusing, isn't it? It's also not a concept you could start out with. You almost need to follow each idea one step at a time so you can slowly process this in such a way that it starts to make more sense.

What's even more fascinating is that the great philosopher, Plato, also had some very similar ideas on the nature of soul, spirit and body. He even tried to express them in drawings using 3 boxes like I've done above. Perhaps these ideas have some overlap in a certain way. It's almost like another layer to the nesting dolls concept where we try to imagine the Triune nature of God, and then try to conceive of the three-fold nature of Christ-in-us, and then try to wrestle with the three coequal yet separate ideas of soul, spirit and body (or perhaps we might say "soul, mind and body").

Still, this is the radical notion that naturally flows out of the initial concept that we are all in Christ and Christ is in all of us. Because, at least in my case, the idea that I, alone, as an individual person, am in Christ—who is in the Father, and who is also in me—takes some time to fully wrap my mind around. But, once it does begin to sink in that this miraculous connection is true for me, I must then stop and consider that, if it's true for me, then it's true of you, and every single other person in the Universe who has ever lived or will ever live.

The reality we need to accept is this: We are all **one** in Christ who makes us all **one**.

The implications of this Oneness are quite mind-blowing, aren't they? I know that it took me a long time to re-orient myself to these ideas and to take time to consider the implications of it.

One day, as I was meditating on this concept, I realized that I could now say, along with Jesus, "Keith is in the Father, and you are in me, and I am in all of you."

Does that sound blasphemous to your ears? I know it did to mine the first time I said them out loud. But, if this is all true; if this is the reality that Jesus wants us to realize, then there is no separation between me and Christ, or between me and you, or between you and everyone else. So, it's not scandalous at all to affirm, as Jesus does, that we are in the Father, and the Father is in us, we are in one another. Because we are all one in Christ who is one with all of us.

If that's too much for you to take in right now, I can sympathize with you. However, we're not quite done yet. There's a bit more to unravel, and unwrap, if you're up for it.

The next layer of this rabbit hole, for me, was when I began to study some of the implications in the realm of Quantum Science. In my previous book, *Sola Mysterium*, we talked about how the universe is composed entirely of a unified field, which implies that everything is connected to everything else. We explored the notion that seemingly separate objects are actually just different expressions of the one, continuous, ubiquitous quantum energy field; meaning that there is no separation between us, or anything else. We used the analogy of how an unlimited number of flames could be produced from a single fire, and how we may perceive each flame as an individual one, but that, in reality, all flame was the one flame. Another analogy might be to say that every drop we take out of the ocean is still that entire ocean in a single drop, or a multitude of drops.

All of this culminates in an even more radical realization that the Universe itself is not a "great machine" as some scientists once assumed, but, as famed Physicist, Sir James Jean proclaimed:

> "Mind [consciousness] no longer appears to be an accidental intruder into the realm of matter...we ought rather to hail it [consciousness] as the creator and governor of the realm of matter."[1]

Consciousness, then, is the single unifying force in the Universe, according to the latest discoveries in quantum physics. You and I might call that "God."

This same consciousness is shared by everyone, everywhere, and—in ways we are only now beginning to wrap our minds around—makes us all **one**.

Are you still with me? I know this is a lot to take in all at once, and all in a single chapter of a book, so it's okay if it's not entirely computing for you right now. These are ideas that took me several months, even years, to process. To be honest, I'm still wrestling with these concepts on a daily basis, so I understand if it's a bit too much too soon for you.

For what it's worth, I think this is exactly the same process that the Apostle Paul went through, because in one of his very first epistles, Paul writes to the church in Galatia and says something pretty radical:

> "There is neither Jew nor Greek, there is neither slave nor free,
> there is no male and female, *for you are all one in Christ Jesus.*"
> [Gal. 3:28; emphasis mine]

At first blush, it appears that Paul has arrived at the same conclusion we have. But, in this earlier epistle, he seems to still be grappling with the same question I was a few years ago: Are all in Christ? Because just before this he says: *"For as many of you as were baptized into Christ have put on Christ."* [v. 27]

So, while Paul seems to have the right idea—that all who are in Christ are one in Christ—he still isn't convinced yet that this applies to everyone, everywhere.

However, fast-forward a bit and you'll see that Paul starts to come around to this notion that Christ's Oneness extends even beyond the confines of the Christian community when he addresses those idol-worshipping pagans in Athens by affirming to them something fairly radical:

"*The God who made the world and everything in it,* being Lord of heaven and earth, does not live in temples made by man, nor is he served by human hands, as though he needed anything, since he *himself gives to all mankind life and breath and everything.* And he made from one man every nation of mankind to live on all the face of the earth, having determined allotted periods and the boundaries of their dwelling place, that they should seek God, and perhaps feel their way toward him and find him. Yet *he [God] is actually not far from each one of us, for 'In him we live and move and have our being';* as even some of your own poets have said, *'For we are indeed his offspring.'*" [Acts. 17:24-28; emphasis mine]

This is an astounding proclamation for an evangelist to make, isn't it? The God who made everything is near to you, blesses you so that you may seek after God, and is the one in whom we all live and move and have our being. Where is the conditional statement to qualify who is in Christ or not? Where is the notion that those without Christ are separated from God's love? It's just not there.

So, it seems that Paul, like many other authors and theologians, had to process things and rethink his ideas over time. Perhaps he would have liked to go back and revise his earlier letter to the Galatians when he told them that it was only those who were baptized into Christ who were qualified to experience oneness?

Perhaps, in some ways, he did exactly that. Because, much later on, in one of Paul's final epistles written to the Colossians, he affirms something similar to what he said when he wrote to the church in Galatia, but with one fairly surprising addition:

"Here there is not Greek and Jew, circumcised and uncircumcised, barbarian, Scythian, slave, free; *but Christ is all, and in all.*" [Col. 3:11][2]

Notice that, again, he affirms that there is no longer any Greek or Jew, slave or free, as he did earlier in his letter to the Galatians, but now he adds the intriguing phrase: *"...but Christ is all and in all,"* which implies something radically different.

If Christ is all, and is in all, then there is no separation between Greek and Jew, slave or free, male or female, or between Christian and Non-Christian. Christ is simply *"all and in all,"* and as he says in another later epistle to the Ephesians, *"Christ fills everything in every way,"* leaving out the possibility of any separation whatsoever.

This means we can no longer continue to talk to God as if God is not entirely intertwined with our very being. We cannot keep thinking of God as a person, or as an individual who exists somewhere other than everywhere at all times.

Having said all of this, it's probably a good idea to clarify something further in this train of thought regarding our oneness with God and with Christ and with one another. When I use the terms Jesus and Christ interchangeably I realize that can cause some unintentional confusion, But I didn't want to try to explain this concept without first establishing the necessary concept of our Oneness with God and one another. So, now that we've come this far I should probably point out that when we speak about Jesus we are talking about a human being who was born roughly two thousand years ago and that when we speak of Christ we are speaking of an eternal Logos that preexisted for all eternity alongside Godself. Yes, the Christ was in Jesus and Jesus was an embodiment of Christ. We could even say that Jesus was perhaps one of the purest and most exceptional incarnations of the Christ we've encountered throughout history. But Jesus was not the only expression of Christ in our world. Because, as we've seen, Christ fills everything in every way. That means

Christ was present long before Jesus was born, and Christ continues to abide in many forms throughout all creation to this very moment.

We'll talk more in depth about this concept in an upcoming chapter, so if you're not fully comfortable with this idea, that's okay. I just wanted to plant the seed in your mind to allow you to consider this idea before we get to it later on in the book.

So, before we go any further, let's spend some more time talking and thinking about Jesus.

"All mature spirituality, in one sense or another, is about letting go and un-learning."

RICHARD ROHR

Chapter 5

THERE'S SOMETHING ABOUT JESUS

TAKE A MOMENT TO let everything we've discussed so far into yourself. Let it permeate your consciousness. Let it percolate and steep.

Allow yourself to breathe in and let it out slowly.

We've challenged a lot of our assumptions. We've asked questions that lead us to doubt so much of what we thought we knew about God, and about humanity.

If God isn't what we thought, and if Christ is more than Jesus, then what does all of this mean for you and me?

To be honest, I really don't have the answers. Even as I write this chapter, I'm uncertain about so many things. What I share with you here are my own questions, my own doubts. The ideas I'm trying to articulate here are fairly new in my mind.

Still, these questions are worth asking, and the mystery is worth exploring, even if we're not totally sure where we'll end up when it's all said and done.

Hopefully you feel the same way. I know these ideas can be scary for some of us, or confusing. My hope is to be as gentle and as thoughtful as possible as we unseal these little envelopes of light one at a time.

So, I think we need to talk about Jesus a little at this point. For many of us, Jesus is the one thing we cling to when everything else fades away. We can question the Bible because we recognize it was written by men thousands of years ago and translated by committees with doctrinal agendas and religious blind spots. Most of us can question doctrines like Eternal Conscious

Torment, and Penal Substitutionary Atonement Theory, and the End Times Rapture, and pretty much anything else; anything except for Jesus.

Why is that? I think it's because Jesus is the one person who has never failed us. Pastors and Bible Teachers have failed us. Denominations have failed us. Church communities have failed us. Individual Christians have hurt us and lied to us and manipulated us for their own benefit. But Jesus? Jesus has never lied to us. Jesus has never hurt us. Jesus has never disappointed us. In fact, it's when we return to those red letters in the Gospels that we find peace, and comfort; hope and forgiveness; joy and light.

I don't know about you, but whenever I read the Sermon on the Mount, my heart skips a beat; my breathing slows down; the anxiety and uncertainty of life fades into the background.

When I read the words of Jesus, I can almost hear his calming voice in my ear, reminding me to trust God, to put my hope in the power of love, to extend mercy to those who need it most, to rest in God's care, to believe things are going to be alright no matter what I'm going through.

Jesus was who I fell in love with all those years ago as a young boy sitting in the pew at the Lighthouse Freewill Baptist Church in Eagle Pass, Texas. Somehow, Jesus was the answer to every question swirling within my heart—questions I didn't even know I had.

When his words settled into the core of my being and scattered seeds of acceptance, and welcome, an inner realization of belonging to the mysterious Abba Father who had always resonated deep within began to permeate my being. I just knew that when I heard the words of Jesus I wanted to hear more. I wanted to know more. I wanted to sit down at his feet and listen. I wanted to crawl up into his lap and lay my head against his chest to hear the beating of his heart in rhythm with my own.

My entire connection with God is through Jesus. It's never been through my church, or through a book, or any doctrine or denominational associations. No, Jesus is my primary touchstone to the Divine. Nothing else has ever come close. I don't believe anything else ever will.

There is a gentle wisdom to Jesus, isn't there? No one else I've ever encountered is so compassionate and insightful, winsome, and patient, loving and kind, as Jesus is. His questions pierce through the veil of doubt. His parables expose the hidden depths of understanding. His example inspires us to be better human beings; to serve better, to love better; to live intentionally, give sacrificially, and trust God with complete abandon.

Jesus is everything I wish I was. He is everything I want to be. Jesus is my blueprint for living this life to the fullest.

So, I cannot let go of Jesus. It would be like letting go of my own soul or forsaking my own existence. Without Jesus, there is no reality for me. Without Jesus I have no connection to or relationship with God.

But that doesn't mean that no one else can have a relationship with God without Jesus. For others, their connection might be another teacher, or another avenue that I just can't imagine or relate to.

It could be that their connection with God—although it may have another name or different expression than I'm familiar with—is exactly the same as what Jesus is for me. They may not use the name "Jesus" or even say "God" when they describe their faith experience, but that's okay. Our differences in religious terminology do not indicate a fundamental difference in the quality or reality of our spiritual experience.

That makes me wonder, when I talk about the ways in which Jesus facilitates my understanding of, and experiences with, God, if there are layers to that relationship that I haven't considered before.

For example, if letting go of Jesus would be like letting go of my own soul, as I said above, then does that suggest that Jesus [or Christ] and my own soul are somehow intertwined? Could it possibly mean that my soul and Christ are essentially the same? Or, when I say that Jesus is the only way I have relationship with God, does that mean that the Christ in me is what connects me to God? Or is it the part of me that is God?

Hold on a minute. I know that last part probably shocked you. What do I mean by "the part of me that is God?" As Christians we're often warned not to cross that line, aren't we? God is God and we are not. But, with everything

43

we've talked about so far, why would we fear exploring the idea that our connection with God goes beyond the concept of separation between human and Divine?

Isn't that the main objection? Aren't we afraid of losing something special about God as being "not human" and of recognizing something in ourselves as "not God"?

To be honest, I'm starting to see that this fear, and that way of thinking about God, is part of the illusion of separation between us and God. We continually want to differentiate ourselves from God. God is "up there" and we are "down here." We still struggle with the idea of "Immanuel" or "God with us," and we're not entirely comfortable with the concept of "Christ in us" as the hope of glory, or with the idea that we are the new incarnation of Christ on earth, as God lives God's life in us and through us.

But, this is the message of Jesus at its core. We've fought against it and resisted it for so long, but it's right there, in plain sight, for any of us to see it, but many of us would really rather not see it.

We've had it drilled into us for so long: God must be God. We must be weak, sinful human beings, and never the twain shall meet.

At best we may think of ourselves as "God's children" or at worst, "God's greatest disappointment." At least, that's what I was always taught to believe. But lately, I've really started to question all of that, and the more I question, the more I feel compelled to rethink everything I thought I knew about God from the inside out. Honestly, I really think my ideas about God have been flawed from the beginning and now need to be reconsidered, and in many cases, totally revised.

That's where I am now, at least. I know I keep repeating this, but It's not like I have this all figured out. I still hold loosely to my beliefs and I'm learning to embrace the mystery of the Divine as I fumble my way through these new ways of thinking about God and of myself.

But embracing this mystery is really a huge part of why it's so necessary for me to ask these questions, and to chase these theological rabbits down the proverbial rabbit hole, no matter where it might lead me.

When I think about Jesus and my relationship with him, am I really experiencing a relationship with Christ? Am I transferring my ideas about the person of Jesus as a wise teacher and an embodiment of God's character into my conception of Christ? Or, is it more accurate to say that, through Jesus, I have a connection and an experience of God's presence through the indwelling Christ? In other words, the same Christ that filled and informed Jesus is the same Christ that fills and informs me now.

I've already deconstructed my views about the Incarnation of Christ and embraced the notion that it is "Christ in me" that must be understood and experienced in order to fully enter the Kingdom of God. I have accepted the idea that what was true of Christ is now true of me and that we are all filled with the fullness of Christ who fills everything in every way. I've embraced the notion that we are the new incarnation of Christ in the world today.

But now I need to really stop and think about what all of that actually means. My curiosity has been stirred. I think it's really important to try to explore as much of this as I possibly can.

Don't you feel the same way? I hope so.

That's where we want to go next.

"God is love. We cannot see love, nor grasp any comprehension of what love is, except as love is clothed with a form. All the love in the universe is God... God, the source of our existence every moment, is not simply omnipotent (all-powerful); He is omnipotence (all power). He is not alone omniscient (all-knowing); He is omniscience (all knowledge). He is not only omnipresent, but more—omnipresence. God is not a being having qualities, but He is the good itself."

H. EMILIE CADY

Chapter 6

THEORETICAL LOGOS

It might be worth taking some time to explore what we mean when we say that Christ is the "Logos" of God, as suggested in the first chapter of John's Gospel before we go much further.

The passage in question reads like this:

> "In the beginning was the Word, and the Word was with God, and the Word was God" (John 1:1).

Some of us were raised to understand that enigmatic passage in John's first chapter as if it's saying something about the Bible. The "Word of God" is quite often used as a reference to the Scriptures, and therefore, we're told, John must be trying to tell us something about the eternal nature of God's Holy Bible. But that's not at all what's being said. If it were, then the first chapter of John would read like this: "In the beginning was the Bible, and the Bible was with God, and the Bible was God."

To be fair, there are more than a few Christians who actually do teach this and believe this. They've made the Gospel about the Bible rather than about Christ.

The reality is that the "Word of God" in this passage is never once described as being written down anywhere. So, whatever it's saying, it's not anything to do with the Bible.

In the Greek, the term for "Word of God" we read in our English Bibles is actually the word "Logos," and it's much more nuanced than many of us realize.

As a Philosophy minor in college, I fell in love with the ideas I discovered from people like Socrates, Plato and Aristotle, and especially later on when I came across Christian philosophers like Hegel and Kierkegaard. But long before philosophers like these ever sat down to think about ultimate reality, there was one philosopher—Heraclitus (535–475 B.C.E.)—who laid some foundational groundwork for ideas that would come to be influential in the study of wisdom, and theology.

Specifically, it was Heraclitus who was perhaps the first to write about the Logos as the guiding principle for reality. As he understood it, the Logos was the principle by which all things arise, as he says it:

> "Things which are put together are both whole and not whole (and are) brought together and taken apart in harmony, and out of harmony; one thing arises from all things and all things arise from one thing."

In spite of the Logos being the principle of our collective, underlying reality, Heraclitus says most of us are totally unaware that it exists. As he explains:

> "Men have no comprehension of the Logos, as I've described it, just as much after they hear about it as they did before they heard about it."

This seems to echo what Réne Girard says about his Mimetic Theory; an underlying principle of human behavior and experience that lies just under the surface of our comprehension, in spite of the fact that it informs nearly every action and choice that we make on a daily basis.

Heraclitus also suggests that the Logos that guides us also remains largely invisible to us:

> "Even though all things occur according to the Logos, men seem to have no experience [of it] whatsoever. Even when they experience the words and deeds which I use to explain (human nature)...the rest of mankind are just as unconscious of what they do while awake as they are of what they do while sleeping."

So, what is the Logos according to Heraclitus? Is it love, or God, community? No. It's violence. Because, to him, the most common human activity throughout all of history is conflict. As he says:

> "It is necessary to understand that war is common, strife is customary, and all things happen because of strife and necessity."

Yet when John chooses to open his Gospel story with this statement about the Logos, he must certainly be aware of what Heraclitus has argued previously regarding the guiding principle that underlies all human activity.

Up to this point in the ancient world, philosophers had assumed that Heraclitus was correct; that violence and war guide the human race. But John wants to suggest something quite different. He wants to remix this prevailing wisdom and argue that the true guiding principle is not conflict, but Christ; not violence, but love.

Unsurprisingly, it is philosopher Réne Girard who points this out to us:

"The Johannine Logos is foreign to any kind of violence. It is therefore forever expelled, an absent Logos that never has had any direct determining influence over human cultures. These cultures are based on the Heraclitean Logos, the Logos of expulsion, the Logos of violence, which, if it is not recognized, can provide the foundation of a culture. The Johannine Logos discloses the truth of violence by having itself expelled. First and foremost, John's Prologue undoubtedly refers to the Passion. But in a more general way, the misrecognition of the Logos and mankind's expulsion of it discloses one of the foundational principles of human culture."

So, what we have here is a collision of underlying principles. Before the Christ Logos entered the world, there was already one operating here—the Logos that Heraclitus describes which is violence and conflict. God's Logos is the true Logos. The Logos described by Heraclitus is real, but it's not the pure underlying principle of the universe. It's more like a counterfeit Logos that humanity created on its own without regard for God's original Logos which is defined by self-giving love (kenosis).

In his book, *The Jesus-Driven Life*, author and theologian Michael Hardin explains all of this in much greater detail:

"Girard is saying that when the principle of nonviolence entered the world of violence it could not be tolerated. The true Logos comes from God...Human culture, founded and maintained by conflict will have nothing to do with the founding principle that is forgiving, reconciliatory, and compassionate. Jesus is the rejected revealer of the reality that his Abba is nonviolent, non-retaliatory, and non-scapegoating...In human culture, the Logos of war and death is preferred to the true Logos who is life and light."[1]

So, when the true Logos of God (Divine Love) entered the World and encountered the false Logos of Man (Violence) the inevitable result was that God's Logos of Love was violently attacked and killed by the guiding principle of violence that permeates our reality. But, in that violence, the Logos of Love was revealed to overcome the Logos of War and the emptiness of our world's false Logos was exposed once and for all.

The Logos of God—expressed in the self-giving love of Christ—was proven to be far superior to the self-destructive Logos of War.

Sophia and Logos

Author and theologian Marcus Borg takes another perspective on the meaning and purpose of this Logos metaphor which I find quite fascinating. In fact, when I first encountered Borg's thesis roughly 7 or 8 years ago, it nearly caused my faith to implode.

So, before I get into this, I want to make sure I prepare you for what we're about to discuss. It might feel as if your understanding of Christ is being undermined or threatened. I know it felt that way to me at the time. The implications of Borg's ideas about the Logos stirred so much fear in my heart that I thought I might be close to losing my faith in Jesus entirely. Without the tender wisdom from my wife, Wendy, to help me walk through the ideas presented, I feel as if I really might have been close to seeing my connection with Christ completely severed and my theological worldview crumble.

I'll do my best to introduce these ideas with as much gentleness and compassion as I possibly can, because I know how frightening and painful they were for me to consider at the time. Still, that being said, I cannot guarantee that you won't also feel the same existential crisis of faith that I experienced when I first heard these ideas.

If you're already feeling some anxiety over this, or if at any time in the following paragraphs you begin to feel uneasy, please feel free to skip ahead to the next section below this. You have every right to guard your heart and take things as slowly as you need to.

So, here's what Marcus Borg said about the Logos and Sophia:

> "There is a...meaning as well...that is foundational for understanding the early Christian movement's language about Jesus as the wisdom of God. In Jewish wisdom literature, wisdom is often personified in female form as "the Wisdom Woman" (Sophia)...

> "This personification first developed in the opening chapters of Proverbs...'Wisdom [Sophia] cries out in the street; in the squares she raises her voice. At the busiest corner she cries out; at the entrance of the city gates she speaks...I will pour out my thoughts [my Spirit] to you, I will make my words known to you."[2]

What Borg points out is that this language more than suggests that Sophia is the personification of God. There are numerous examples provided in his book, *Meeting Jesus Again For The First Time*, where Borg makes his case that everything said about Sophia in Proverbs and other Jewish texts is synonymous with the Logos described in John's Gospel.

For example, in Proverbs 8:1 to 9:6 there is an extended speech by Sophia given where she speaks of herself as the source of truth, insight and strength (analogous to the Way, the Truth and the Life language used by Jesus in John chapter 14), and later in this passage she speaks of her role in the Creation of the Universe by claiming that she was with God in the beginning before anything was made and that not only was Sophia with God from the beginning, she was co-creator with God:

> "When God established the heavens, I was there...When God marked out the foundations of the Earth, I was beside God as a master worker." [Prov. 8:27-30]

You may no doubt notice the striking similarities between this passage and the first chapter of John's Gospel where he says of the Logos:

> "In the beginning was the Logos, and the Logos was with God, and the Logos was God. [The Logos] was with God in the beginning. Through [the Logos] all things were made; without [the Logos] nothing was made that has been made." [v.1-3]

I've replaced the word "him" in the above passages from John's Gospel because the reference is to the masculine of the term Logos and not necessarily to Jesus. If the passage had been a reference to Sophia, for example, those references would have said, "her" or "she" because of the use of the feminine term, Sophia. So, there may be some confusion for us when we read John's Gospel if we mix up the references to the masculine word Logos being personified as "he", with the person of Jesus. Later, yes, John does eventually say that this Logos "became flesh and dwelt among us," but that is the first time Jesus appears in the prologue. Everything up to that point is a reference to the idea or concept of Logos.

In Proverbs 9: 2-5, Sophia invites us to: "Come, eat of my bread and drink of the wine I have mixed," which conjures images of Jesus at the last supper offering his disciples bread and wine that he refers to as his own body and blood.

As Borg continues:

> "The Jewish personification of wisdom as Sophia and the attribution to her of divine qualities becomes even more developed in two intertestamental books—Sirach and the Wisdom of Solomon. In Sirach, written around 180 B.C., Sophia again speaks of her origin in God: "From eternity, in the beginning, God created me and for eternity I shall not cease to be."

> "She speaks of her presence everywhere: "I came forth from the mouth of the Most High [the Word of God], and covered the earth like a mist [reference to the Holy Spirit in Genesis]. I dwelt in the highest heavens, and my throne was in a pillar of cloud [similar to the image of God travelling with the Israelites during the Exodus]. Alone I compassed the vault of heaven and traversed the depths of the abyss. Over waves of the sea, over all the earth, and over every people and nation have I held sway."[3]

Borg also mentions that Sophia is described as having all of the attributes of God in the Wisdom of Solomon which was written near the time of Jesus where she is spoken of as:

> "...a spirit that is intelligent, holy, unique, manifold, subtle, mobile, clear, unpolluted, distinct, invulnerable, loving the good, keen, irresistible beneficent, humane, steadfast, sure, free from anxiety, all-powerful, overseeing all, and penetrating through all spirits...a breath of the power of God and a pure emanation of the glory of the Almighty..a reflection of eternal light...she can do all things...she renews all things."[4]

Borg's point is that this personification of an idea, or a principle, was already well-established in ancient Jewish scripture and literature long before John wrote his Gospel. In fact, it's nearly impossible to assume that John was unaware of this personification of Sophia in the Hebrew tradition when he penned his words which essentially replace the familiar term for wisdom with the new idea, Logos.

Now, you may be wondering why any of that nearly sent me off the deep end a few years ago. Maybe you read that now and think, "Yeah, so what? Why all the angst over something like this?"

Well, truthfully, none of this bothers me today. But a few years ago, long before I could even grasp the idea that Christ was in everyone and everyone was in Christ, these ideas put me into a theological tailspin. I think it was because, at the time, the idea of separating Jesus from the Christ was just too much for me to handle. I needed Jesus to be the one who was with God in the beginning. I couldn't handle the idea of Jesus being fully human and the Christ in him being the same Christ that is in everyone.

But, for some of you, this might bother you the way it bothered me. If so, feel free to set these ideas aside until you're ready to process them at a later date. Even if you're not troubled by these ideas, perhaps you can at least sympathize with my momentary theological crisis at the time; as someone who was not quite ready to rethink my ideas about Jesus and the Christ in such radical ways.

"As you start to walk on the way, the way appears."

RUMI

Chapter 7

WHEN CHRIST FILLED EVERYTHING IN EVERY WAY

I RECENTLY CAME ACROSS an exceptionally breath-taking paragraph written by Athanasius around 325 AD, where he says:

> "*For He [Christ] was not, as might be imagined, circumscribed in the body, nor, while present in the body, was He absent elsewhere; nor, while He moved the body, was the universe left void of His working and Providence; but,* thing most marvelous, Word as He was, so far from being contained by anything, *He rather contained all things Himself; and just as while present in the whole of Creation, He is at once distinct in being from the universe, and present in all things by His own power*—giving order to all things, and *over all and in all revealing His own providence, and giving life to each thing and all things,* including the whole without being included, but being in His own Father alone wholly and in every respect—*thus, even while present in a human body and Himself quickening it, He was, without inconsistency, quickening the universe as well, and was in every process of nature,* and was outside the whole, and while known from the body by His works, He was none the less manifest from the working of the universe as well." [emphasis added]

As with our previous chapter, this quotation affirms in no uncertain terms that Christ was both in the body of Jesus and fully present in the entire universe at the very same time. No separation. No division. All the fullness of Christ filled everything in every way, and still does.

This is why I so appreciate the work of the mystics who try to help us understand that Christ is all and in all. So, for example, when I hear people like Richard Rohr describe our connection with Christ in these same terms, it really encourages me:

> "The first two thousand years of Christianity have largely struggled with Jesus of Nazareth...and the reason we didn't deal with Jesus of Nazareth very well is that we didn't know that Christ isn't his last name. We just put those words "Jesus Christ" together and we fail to read...the first chapter of Ephesians, the first chapter of Colossians, the first chapter of John's Gospel, the first paragraph of the letter to the Hebrews, and the first paragraph of the first letter from John [1 John]—all of them the first.

> "These five books of the New Testament they all say very clearly that Christ existed from all eternity. [But] Jesus existed only [in the last] 2,000 years. So, right there we should say, 'Wow! We're talking about two realities.' But we just lump them together [and say], 'I believe in Jesus Christ!'

> "Up to now most Christians, at best, and on a good day, believe in Jesus. But they've lost his whole cosmic dimension. They've lost his whole 'larger than history' dimension. We've pulled him out of the blessed Trinity, if I can talk theologically, and we've made him back into God the Father for all practical purposes. [Therefore], most Christian doctrine is not [truly]

Trinitarian...we haven't really worked with that mystery [to realize] that God is more a verb than a noun. God is an endless outpouring of love between the Three. God is a dynamism. God is a relationship.

"There's a part of God that is formless, we call that The Father, and there's a part of God that is form, and we call that Jesus—he took shape that we could see—and there's a part of God that is energy, relationship and community between the Father and the Son [the Spirit]...and we are standing in the middle of that giving and that relationship.

"Now, the Christ existed from all Eternity...[and] at least in terms of the Universe that we know, we can measure to some degree, that this manifestation began 14.6 billion years ago, when God decided to show Godself...and I would call that the original incarnation.

"Suddenly we've got a very different notion of God that's much bigger, more grand, much more universal and more patient than we imagined.

"We say, 'Who is this God?' and that's the Christ Mystery. When Spirit began to reveal itself through matter—when matter and spirit became one—that's the Christ. That's the Christ Mystery."[1]

Richard Rohr enunciates the very same perspective that Athanasius expressed in 325 AD, and he and many others are also beginning to grasp at this same understanding of Christ as a cosmic reality that transcends theology.

Yet, sadly, when these mystics attempt to affirm the notion that Christ is not separate from us, they are called heretics and false teachers by the gatekeepers of theology who seem to want to have their cake and eat it, too. Meaning, they love the idea of an exalted, transcendent Christ who is not "contained by anything, but contains all things Himself," but, at the same time, they reject the notion that Christ fills everything—and everyone—in every way.

Yes, they want a Christ who is lifted up, high and above the rest of Creation, but they do not want one that freely shares the Divine nature with every one of us.

For example, I recently heard noted Christian philosopher and apologist, Dr. Douglas Groothuis, suggest that while Athanasius was entirely Orthodox in suggesting what we read above, modern theologians like Richard Rohr are dangerously heretical for teaching the exact same thing.

Here's what Groothuis said when asked to compare Rohr and Athanasius on the question of "Christ in all things":

> "I hope that Richard Rohr is saying what Athanasius said, but my reading of both of them would say that Athanasius is fully Orthodox, and he defends a unique and distinct incarnation. Rohr says the Creation was the first Incarnation [of Christ] and that the Incarnation continues. You never find Athanasius using that kind of language."[2]

Dr. Groothuis somehow refuses to see that both Rohr and Athanasius affirm the same ideas: That Christ was and is always present within all creation. He seems to dismiss not only what Athanasius says in the quotation above about Christ being incarnated in Jesus and present everywhere else in the Universe at the same time, but he also manages to gloss over what Paul says in Philippians, Colossians and Ephesians regarding Christ's oneness with all things.

The reality is that Athanasius, like Rohr, affirms that:

> "[Christ] was, so far from being contained by anything, He rather contained all things Himself; and just as while present in the whole of Creation, He is at once distinct in being from the universe, and present in all things by His own power—giving order to all things, and over all and in all...and was in every process of nature..."

My question for someone like Dr. Groothuis would be this: When did Christ become all and in all? When did Christ fill everything in every way?

The position seems to be that it's heresy to suggest that the Creation itself is the first incarnation of Christ, as Rohr and others affirm. Yet, if this is so, then at what point did Christ fill all things in every way? If not at the creation of the universe—and previous to the physical incarnation of Christ in the person of Jesus of Nazareth—then when? Did Christ fill all things in every way only after the incarnation of Jesus? If so, then doesn't that suggest that Christ was somehow created, or that Christ didn't come into being until the First Century, after the birth of Jesus?

Honestly, if that is what Groothuis is suggesting, then that certainly qualifies more as heresy since it directly contradicts everything we've seen up to this point from both Jesus and from the epistles of Paul.

If Christ existed from all eternity, and if Christ fills everything in every way, then Christ has always done so. So, if Christ inhabited space and time and matter and energy from the very beginning, even before the beginning of all things, then Christ was in all of creation long before Christ was in Jesus. There's no way around it. Either Christ entered the creation through the incarnation of Jesus, or the Christ was always present in the whole of Creation prior to the birth of Jesus.

Both Athanasius and Rohr affirm the latter; that Christ is and always has been present in the Creation from the moment there was a Universe to inhabit. Billions of years before Jesus, there was Christ, and Christ was all and in all.

This is a new concept for many of us. We've mainly assumed that Christ and Jesus were the same thing, and that Christ and Jesus entered the universe at the same time. But perhaps we've been wrong about that? Maybe we need to reconsider that assumption in light of the words of Jesus and Paul and Athanasius and Rohr.

This paradigm shift unlocks a myriad of questions for us. It challenges us to rethink the nature of Christ, and our own nature, and so many other things, all at the same time.

For example, if it were possible for someone to exist apart from, or outside of, Christ, what would hold them together if not Christ? How can someone exist apart from whatever it is that "holds all things together"?

And how could anyone exist without Christ being in them if, by definition, Christ is the one who "fills everything in every way"? How would that even work?

Frankly, it wouldn't. And that's my point. Apologists like Groothuis cannot simply wave their hands and create a version of reality that suits them while affirming Athanasius and denouncing Rohr who happen to both agree on the cosmic nature of Christ.

Honestly, I have to wonder why anyone would attempt to assert that Athanasius never said that "Creation was the first incarnation" when, actually, that is plainly what he does affirm in the passage above?

Perhaps it's easier for some to label Rohr and others like him false teachers and heretics than to say the same of someone like Athanasius who helped formulate the doctrine of the Trinity and presided over the Council of Nicea.

What's more, I believe it's the radical idea that Christ was incarnated in Creation—prior to the incarnation of Christ in the body of Jesus—that carries implications that some theologians simply are not willing to fully accept.

You should ask yourself why any Christian apologist or philosopher would want to reject the notion that Christ is eternal, without beginning or end, and therefore fills everything in every way, as Jesus, and Paul and Athanasius and Rohr all affirm? What's the danger of this idea? What's so scary to them about what this implies for humanity? Is it the idea that we are all in Christ? Is it the possibility that we are all one with Christ and with everyone else? Is it the notion that there really isn't any distinction between Christians and Atheists, men and women, gay and straight, young or old, rich or poor?

What does the concept of separation provide these theologians that they want so desperately to protect it? Isn't it that, if we realized we were all already loved and accepted by God that we'd no longer need them, or any other religion? Isn't it that, without division and separation, we wouldn't need to keep coming back week after week to get forgiven and restored into right relationship to God?

By promoting and protecting the idea of separation between God and mankind, these Christian leaders have found a way to keep us jumping through their hoops to gain something we already have: complete *oneness* with God, and with everyone else!

As long as we accept the idea of separation from God, we will continue to play their games and follow their rules. But, once our eyes are opened and we realize that everyone is already fully intertwined with Christ, there's no need to entertain religious ideas anymore. We're free from their bondage. We're liberated from their attempts to control and manipulate us.

This realization of our Oneness with God, or Christ, and our subsequent entanglement with all living beings in the universe because of that connection, isn't merely an obscure mystical concept that some find hidden in the New Testament. The very same spiritual truth has been expressed throughout a variety of other religious writings and mystical teachings for millennia. Perhaps this is why some find it so threatening.

Even the non-religious skeptical scientists who study Quantum Physics are coming around to the very same conclusion: Consciousness is the ground of all being. The Universe is a giant thought, not a mechanical construction. Everyone, and everything, is connected on a fundamental level that forces us to re-think, and reconsider—*Metanoia!*—every assumption we've ever had about who we are, and what reality is all about.

If God is more than we imagined. If Christ is beyond space and time. If everything in our Universe is knitted together in some mysterious weaving of Divinity and Humanity, then we need to take a step back and reevaluate literally everything we thought we knew about everything.

I hope you're ready for where we're going next. There's more to consider when it comes to understanding our identity in Christ and the nature of reality in light of this cosmic connection we're only beginning to awaken to.

See you in the next chapter.

"God became human so that humans should become God. Only the God who is always already human can become human. Only a humanity that is always already divine can become God."

DAVID BENTLEY HART

Chapter 8

BECOMING CHRIST

I ONCE HAD A wonderful conversation with Father Kenneth Tanner about this idea of how Jesus became the Christ. During our talk, he referenced a quote from our old friend Athanasius who spoke about the Incarnation of Christ being a journey, rather than a single event in time. The idea that was being expressed was that Christ didn't become fully human until Jesus died on the cross and that Jesus didn't become fully Christ until he experienced the resurrection.

Now that really got me thinking and so I started to dig into this quote, and into what other early Church Fathers believed about the Incarnation, and their ideas of Christ, and that led me to study more about what they believed about the process of Deification within humanity.

Here's where this little exploration has taken me so far.

First, we'll start with these quotes from Athanasius who, as a reminder, was the Bishop of Alexandria and lived between 296 and 373 A.D.

> "*The Word was made flesh in order that we might be made gods* ... Just as the Lord, putting on the body, became a man, *so also we men are both deified through his flesh*, and henceforth inherit everlasting life."

"For the Son of God became man so that we might become God."

"He was made human *so that he might make us gods.*"

Now, of course, this teaching isn't unique to Athanasius. In the Gospel of John we see the Lord Jesus Himself quoting from the Old Testament scriptures to show us that God has already said that we are gods:

> "They answered him, "It is not for a good work that we are going to stone you but for blasphemy, because you, being a man, make yourself God." Jesus answered them, *"Is it not written in your Law, 'I said, you are gods'?* If he called them gods to whom the word of God came—and Scripture cannot be broken— do you say of him whom the Father consecrated and sent into the world, 'You are blaspheming,' because I said, 'I am the Son of God'? [John 10:33-36, emphasis mine]

The Apostle Paul picks up on this notion and affirms this in his own epistles, for example, in 2 Corinthians 3:17—18 he says that:

> "...we all, with unveiled faces, beholding the glory of the Lord, *are being transformed into the same image* [of God] from one degree of glory to another."

Paul also said:

> "Now if we are children, then we are heirs—heirs of God and co-heirs with Christ, if indeed we share in his sufferings *in order that we may also share in his glory.*" [Romans 8:17]

And the author of 1 John affirms this also saying:

> "*Beloved, now we are the sons of God*, and it doth not yet appear what we shall be; *but we know that, when He shall appear, we shall be like Him*; for we shall see Him as He is." [1 John 3:2]

So, this transformation is a natural process that was a journey for Jesus to undergo as much as it will be a journey and a process for the rest of us.

Apparently, this teaching about the Deification of humanity can be found as early as the writings of Irenaeus, a Greek leader in the early Church of Lyons (130-202 A.D.) who said that God had *"become what we are, that He might bring us to be even what He is Himself."*

Irenaeus also said:

> "Do we cast blame on him [God] because *we were not made gods from the beginning, but were at first created merely as men, and then later as gods?* Although God has adopted this course out of his pure benevolence, that no one may charge him with discrimination or stinginess, he declares, *"I have said, Ye are gods; and all of you are sons of the Most High."* ... For it was necessary at first that nature be exhibited, *then after that what was mortal would be conquered and swallowed up in immortality."*

Deification or Divinization of Christians was understood to be a process that took place during the receiving of the Eucharist. This was widely taught by early Church Fathers like Gregory of Nyssa and Cyril of Alexandria.

However—and we need to stress this here—this teaching never crossed the line into suggesting that Christians become God [with a capital G]. It only suggested that those who were in Christ were being made in the image of

God to become like God. More specifically, they believed that Christians were those who were literally Incarnating Christ in their own bodies due to the indwelling and transforming Spirit of Christ that lived within them. Sort of like the doctrine of Sanctification turned up to eleven.

This doctrine was not an isolated one. In fact, there were numerous references to this process of Deification or Divinization of believers in the writings of the early Christians, for example:

Clement of Alexandria (150—215 A.D.)

"Yea, I say, *the Word of God became a man so that you might learn from a man how to become a god* ... if one knows himself, he will know God, *and knowing God will become like God* ... His is beauty, true beauty, for it is God, *and that man becomes a god, since God wills it.* So Heraclitus was right when he said, *'Men are gods, and gods are men'*..."..."...he who obeys the Lord and follows the prophecy given through him ... *becomes a god while still moving about in the flesh.*'"

Justin Martyr (100–165 A.D.)

"[In the beginning] *men were made like God*, free from suffering and death," [and now are] "*deemed worthy of becoming gods* and of having power to become sons of the highest."

*Even the great **Augustine of Hippo (354–403 A.D.)*** said this:

> "*But he himself that justifies also deifies,* for by justifying he makes sons of God. 'For he has given them power to become the sons of God' [referring to John 1:12]. *If then we have been made sons of god, we have also been made gods... To make human beings gods, He was made man who was God...*"

And it doesn't end there. Not by a long shot.

Theophilus of Antioch (120–190 A.D.)

> "For if He had made him [mankind] immortal from the beginning, He would have made him God. Again, if He had made him mortal, God would seem to be the cause of his death. Neither, then, immortal nor yet mortal did He make him, but, as we have said above, capable of both; so that if he should incline to the things of immortality, keeping the commandment of God, *he should receive as reward from Him immortality, and should become God...*"

Hippolytus of Rome (170–235 A.D.)

> "And you shall be a companion of the Deity, and a co-heir with Christ, no longer enslaved by lusts or passions, and never again wasted by disease. *For you have become God*: for whatever sufferings you underwent while being a man, these He gave to you, because you were of mortal mould, but whatever it

is consistent with God to impart, these God has promised to bestow upon you, *because you have been deified, and begotten unto immortality.*"

"*If, therefore, man has become immortal, he will also be God.* And if he is made God by water and the Holy Spirit after the regeneration of the laver he is found to be also joint-heir with Christ after the resurrection from the dead."

Gregory of Nyssa (335–395 A.D.)

"*Since the God who was manifested infused Himself into perishable humanity for this purpose, viz. that by this communion with Deity mankind might at the same time be deified...*"

Maximus the Confessor (580–662 A.D.)

"Nothing in theosis is the product of human nature, for nature cannot comprehend God. It is only the mercy of God that has the capacity to endow theosis unto the existing... *In theosis, man (the image of God) becomes likened to God*, he rejoices in all the plenitude that does not belong to him by nature, because the grace of the Spirit triumphs within him, and because God acts in him."

Cyril of Alexandria (376–444 A.D.)

"[H]e came down into our condition solely in order to lead us to his own divine state."

"It follows, therefore, that He Who Is, The One Who Exists, is necessarily born of the flesh, taking all that is ours into himself so that all that is born of the flesh, that is us corruptible and perishing human beings, might rest in him. In short, *he took what was ours to be his very own so that we might have all that was his.*"

"*For we too are sons and gods by grace,* and we have surely been brought to this wonderful and supernatural dignity since we have the Only Begotten Word of God dwelling within us."

Gregory of Nazianzus (329–290 A.D.)

"...*[we] become gods for (God's) sake, since (God) became man for our sake.*"

"[The Spirit of God] pleads even now as Man for my salvation; for He continues to wear the Body which He assumed, *until He make me God by the power of His Incarnation.*"

"Through the medium of the mind he had dealings with the flesh, *being made that God on earth, which is Man: Man and God blended.* They became a single whole, the stronger side predominating, in *order that I might be made God to the same extent that he was made man.*"

Basil of Caesarea (330–379 A.D.)

"*...[for] becoming a god is the highest goal of all*"

St. Thomas Aquinas (1225–1274 A.D.)

"*Now the gift of grace surpasses every capability of created nature, since it is nothing short of a partaking of the Divine Nature*, which exceeds every other nature. And thus it is impossible that any creature should cause grace. *For it is as necessary that God alone should deify, bestowing a partaking of the Divine Nature* by a participated likeness, as it is impossible that anything save fire should enkindle.*"

So, I don't know about you, but that's a lot more support from the early Church Fathers about the Deification of Humanity than I would ever have imagined.

This must mean that it's not entirely out of the question for us, as followers of Christ today, to ask some of these same questions about the notion that we are, in fact, gods.

What's more, if we fail to explore these ideas, it's like we're actually choosing to ignore the implications of the Incarnation or to fully consider the reality of our identity in Christ.

So, just to be perfectly clear, if we begin to ponder the notion that God's intention is to make us all Godlike, this is not heresy. Unless you want to argue that all of these great saints and theologians from the pantheon of Christian history are also heretics, you must concede that the deification of mankind is—without a doubt—an entirely Orthodox way of thinking.

Surprisingly enough, it seems that the idea of becoming god is not only not heretical, it is, in truth, essentially a lost teaching of the early Christian Church; one that we might want to explore a bit further.

Another idea along these lines that really fascinates me is the fact that many early Christian thinkers taught that Christ's journey to becoming fully human culminated in his death, and that Jesus's journey to become fully Christ was culminated in his resurrection.

In other words, this was a process, not an immediate reality. The Christ had to become incarnate by being born, living life, and then suffering and dying. Jesus, the man, had to become the Christ by being filled with the Spirit of God, living a godly life, and, after dying, rise from the dead.

The book of Acts suggests strongly that Jesus did indeed become Christ at his resurrection, as the Apostle Peter said in his Pentecostal sermon:

> "Therefore let all Israel be assured of this: *God has made this Jesus*, whom you crucified, *both Lord and Christ.*" [Acts 2:36]

The implication here is that Jesus "was made...both Lord and Christ," meaning that he was not already Lord or Christ but was made to become Christ at his resurrection.

The Apostle Paul suggests that the Christ did not become fully incarnate until he experienced death on the cross, as expressed in Philippians 2:8-9:

> "And being found in human form, *he [Christ] humbled himself by becoming obedient to the point of death*, even death on a cross. *Therefore, God has highly exalted him and bestowed on him the name that is above every name...*"

These two passages provide the foundation for what became this doctrine of deification as we've already seen above.

What I took away from this intriguing conversation with Fr. Tanner was the amazing parallel of "becoming" for both the Christ and for Jesus of Nazareth. The Christ became human. The human became Christ.

Frankly, it shocked me to realize that the New Testament really does suggest that Jesus was "made the Christ" or that he "became Christ", meaning this was a process, not something that was automatically true at his conception, or his birth.

Not all early Church Fathers understood the Incarnation of Christ this way. Some taught that Jesus became the Christ [which literally means 'the Anointed One'] at his baptism because this was when the Spirit of God was poured out on Jesus and God said, 'This is my Son.'"

Others taught that Jesus became the Christ at his death, and still others, at the resurrection. Either way, there was a pervading notion that Jesus became the Christ over time and through a process of obedience to the Father throughout His life.

So, all of these ideas taken together seem to suggest the possibility that both the Incarnation of Christ in the body of Jesus was a process, and the total revelation of Jesus as the Christ was also a process.

That's what has me reeling: The Incarnation of Christ wasn't complete until Jesus died. Jesus did not fully become the Christ until the resurrection.

That's fascinating stuff, isn't it? So here I am, meditating on how this same process of becoming like Christ is now taking place within me, and you, and all of us, as we are being made new and transformed into the image of Christ; a process that will culminate in our death, and in our own resurrection where we become, inevitably, like Christ.

As my friend Matthew J. Distefano says, *"If God is the Infinite, and we are always becoming more and more like God/Christ, then part of what it means to become god is to always be growing. In other words, [we are] getting to the Infinite with incremental steps, [which is] impossible, [but] that is part of the fun of what it means to be a human who is becoming more and more and more [ad infinitum] like God."*[1]

This is a wonderful observation. It means arriving at our destination may never be complete because God is not a single point or location in space and time. God is Infinite, and so our journey to becoming god is an infinitely long process along the divine journey of becoming. To stop this process is to cease becoming fully human, or fully God.

Another fascinating thing to consider is how Jesus redefines the concept of becoming godlike. For the longest time, humanity thought of God—or really any ancient conception of Divinity—as wielding ultimate power and infinite wisdom; about ruling over the weak and foolish people of earth; about exerting One's perfect will over everyone else on earth. There's a fascinating example of how people in the ancient world imagined what it meant to be godlike found in Acts 12: 21-23 where it says that King Herod *"...put on his royal robes and took his seat upon his royal throne and delivered an ovation to them, and the people shouted, 'The voice of a god, not a man!'"*

The people were dazzled by Herod's majesty and awed by his powerful voice as he sat adorned on his royal throne. To them, this is what God was like. But when Jesus arrives on the scene he's nothing like this. In fact, when we read the Apostle Paul's description of how Jesus never "considered likeness with God something to be grasped, but emptied himself...becoming nothing," in Philippians chapter 2, it's a massive game-changer. Here is a God who let go of all of that power and majesty and decides instead to become like one of us. Not only like one of us, but even lower than us—a slave who bends down and serves us.

That's radical, and totally against the grain of what anyone previously would have imagined God being like.

So, if we're to become like God, it's in the sense that Jesus models for us, not in the ancient image of a being who sits on a throne above creation looking down on everyone and demanding worship and obedience. Ironically, to become like God is to become more humble, like Jesus: to let go of power and to serve others in humility and self-giving love. That's what it means to become Deified. It means to become more Christlike.

So, hopefully all of this creates a sense of curiosity about this mysterious process of Incarnation and Deification. I mean, I can't be the only one who reads these quotes and starts to meditate on the implications, can I? Otherwise, what could it mean to affirm as Jesus and the early church fathers did, that "we are gods" or that we are "made into God"?

The first reflexive response to the notion is to say "You're being prideful." As if what we mean to say is that we are "The One True God" who pre-existed and who created all things out of the breath of His mouth. No, of course not. We are not saying that at all. No one of us is the One God. But, what we are saying is that nothing exists apart from God; that God wears all of creation like a wardrobe and that, without God, creation has no shape or form. There is no part of me that is not part of God and no part of God that is not part of me.

Creation is animated by and inhabited by God. There can be no such thing as creation apart from the God who has become manifested within that creation. So, for me, as part of that creation, to say that there is a part of me that is God, I am affirming that, apart from God, I do not exist. There is a part of me that is God's presence made flesh. God exists, at least in some part, as me.

Where we run into trouble is when we suggest that, apart from me, God does not exist. In other words, to say that God does not exist apart from creation and that without our consciousness, God's consciousness is not conscious, or aware.

That's the fundamental difference between Panentheism and Pantheism. Either God is *in* all Creation, or all Creation *is* God. Are they both true in some sense? Are they mutually exclusive concepts that must be reconciled or evaluated against one another?

Let's try to understand them first.

"Apprehend God in all things, for God is in all things. Every single creature is full of God and is a book about God. Every creature is a word of God."

MEISTER ECKHART

Chapter 9

PANENTHEISM VS. PANTHEISM

LET'S TALK ABOUT SOME of the ways that people tend to think about God in contrast to classical Christian Theism. One way of conceptualizing God is known as Pantheism and the other is called Panentheism.

The link between classical Theism and Panentheism is stronger than the one between Pantheism and Panentheism. Because while Theism wants to argue for a God who maintains a distinct consciousness apart from creation, Panentheism argues that creation itself is an expression of the Divine Consciousness in material form. In other words, God is IN all things, but not—as Pantheism teaches—that God IS all things.

That is the crucial distinction between the two views. By definition, Panentheism is the belief that God [or Christ] permeates all of creation, whereas Pantheism says that all of Creation IS God, in totality. So, it would seem that you either believe that God expresses Godself through the creation, or you believe that God is nothing more and nothing less than the sum total of all creation.

Let's examine these ideas for a moment.

First, we'll start with Pantheism. In this view, God has no separate mind or consciousness or state of being. Every single thing in this Universe is a small piece of the larger reality that they would call "God." Or, to put it another way, "the World [or the Universe] is God."

Theologian John Milbank explains this concept by saying, *"Pantheism is nearer the truth than is Panentheism (even if not quite there). For God is not simply another thing in relation to the world, and the world is not simply another thing in relation to God."*

What he means here is that, to his understanding, God is not in the world and, at the same time, separate from the world. He believes that Panentheism is logically inconsistent for suggesting that God could both inhabit [or incarnate] all of creation and yet still exist apart from this creation. But is he right?

For those who take a hardline non-dualistic approach, this way of thinking might seem accurate. In other words, it seems logically inconsistent to say that we are all one with God, or with Christ—because Christ fills everything in every way—and then to turn around and also affirm that Christ exists apart from us. This seems almost self-refuting.

For example, to go back to the little series of boxes I drew on my napkin which slowly removed the lines separating God and Christ, and then Christ and us, the idea that there is a part of God that is both fully entangled with humanity, and yet, somehow another part of God that is separated from humanity in some way seems to break the entire idea apart. How would we draw such a thing in our napkin series? Does it make sense to say that part of God is one with Christ and with all of us, and all of creation, but, somehow, there's another part of God somewhere over on the side that is not included in that union?

If God and Christ fill everything in every way, and if we are all filled with the fullness of Christ, then how can there be some other parts of God that we are not filled with?

For a Panentheist the answer is that God fills everything in every way, but still maintains a transcendent sense of consciousness in addition to that indwelling aspect of God's being. Or, to put it differently, "God is *in* all things, but God is *not* all things."

Still, these distinctions are not so easy to differentiate. The questions about the ways in which God may [or may not] have a consciousness or state of being apart from the physical reality are not easy to answer. In fact, it may very well be impossible to do so with our limited understanding.

Whereas a Pantheist might say that there is no distinct being known as "God" apart from the individual expressions of God in the physical universe, a Panentheist might suggest that God's consciousness is expressed in the collective consciousness of all things, while, at the same time, having a higher, or separate consciousness apart from creation.

So, in some cases, a Pantheist and a Panentheist might sometimes say almost the same things, but what they mean to communicate might be something drastically different.

Panentheistic Evidence

The ways that we see the character and nature of God being expressed in New Testament documents like the Gospel of John, or Galatians, or Colossians, or Ephesians, etc., are quite Panentheistic. Both God and Christ are often said to inhabit all things, or to have created all things while also holding all things together.

I like the way Richard Rohr says it:

> "All of this creation: that sky, these trees, this vine, they're all a manifestation—not in the same way—I'm not saying they're all god—but they all participate in this one Christ Mystery.

> "Paul understood this. He called it the "Body of Christ" and he was talking about us being a part of this same universal body. Christ is the head, and we are the members. Paul [in 1 Cor.] is already moving out to include people. In Romans 8 he talks about all of creation groaning until it [awakens and] becomes the full "sonship of God." So, it's not just humans.

"Then, he attributes something as ordinary as bread with the Body of Christ, the Eucharist. So, it just keeps moving outward, wherever matter and spirit co-exist."[1]

So, everything we've examined so far points to an emphatically Christian-Panentheistic worldview.

But, if I'm honest, the challenge I find myself in at the moment is to understand the fundamental distinction between God *in* all things versus God *as* all things. Where does Panentheism end and Pantheism begin?

The classical understanding of God—in Judeo-Christian Theism—understands God as essentially the ultimate man. Like human beings, God could be jealous, angry, wrathful, envious and sad. Unlike human beings, however, God is all-knowing, all-powerful, and all-present. God is also eternally existent and without beginning or end.

But I have to wonder, why are so many theologians and philosophers moving away from those traditional concepts of God? Perhaps because the notion of a personal God introduces a set of seemingly insoluble problems like the problem of suffering and evil in the world. Surely a God who is all-knowing, all-powerful, and omni-present would—and should—intervene on behalf of the innocent, or alleviate suffering, or respond swiftly to evil. A truly all-knowing and all-powerful God would certainly never have designed a world like ours where such evil and suffering permeated human experience.

So, the idea that God might not be a personal God has, for some, provided a preferable response to these sorts of questions. What's more, the belief that God is a person might simply be the by-product of the fact that we are persons, and so it's possible that we have merely projected ourselves into the concept of the Divine without realizing it.

On one level, it's difficult for most of us to imagine a being or a person who doesn't have a body. The personal God is somehow both a being and person who is merely a Spirit, without a body of any kind. At least, from the Hebrew perspective, God does not have a body.

In Christianity, that problem was solved by incarnating God into the body of Jesus. Still, a personal God is a separate being from the rest of creation. Oddly enough, once theologians began to really consider the implications of God taking on flesh, it opened up a series of even more complicated ideas that began to sound a lot more like Panentheism, where God [or Christ] was in all things, and before all things, and that all things lived and moved and had their being in God [or Christ], and that everything resonated with the frequency of the Divine presence.

Still, many Christian Panentheists cling to the notion of both a personal God who exhibits human attributes, and at the same time, permeates every aspect of reality everywhere.

But is this possible from a logical standpoint? One might ask, "How can God fill everything in every way, and yet still be a separate being from all Creation at the same time?"

I don't know about you, but the idea of a personal God has always made sense to me. I have always felt that God was someone I could talk to, and relate to. God loved me. God cared about me. God was concerned for my well-being and was aware of my struggles and fears. I could share my thoughts with God and, at least to me, it seemed like God often talked back to me if I was really listening for God's voice.

But the more I reflect on the ideas contained in Pantheism, I can start to see some truth in it, even as I struggle with the idea that God might not have a separate consciousness or being apart from me, or the rest of creation. But I also see some profound truth in Panentheism as well. So, where does that leave me?

Perhaps the reason this is so hard for me to accept Pantheism is because I've always felt a strong connection to God. That connection has always felt personal to me. Even as I begin to consider moving away from the idea of God as a separate being and start to think of God as the Christ which fills everything in every way, I can still accept all of the ways in which the Christ in me is alive and present; how the love of God is always accessible and even how my imagination created a version of that God that I could relate to, talk to, take comfort in, and carry with me.

But now I'm asking different questions. I'm almost fearful of starting to shift away from the idea of a God who is personal. Not that I'm completely comfortable with the concept of God as a big man in the sky who exists apart from myself. But, the more I move closer to the idea of a God, or of Christ, as a being of eternal Consciousness that permeates all things, everywhere, I can also, somehow, relate to that concept.

Whatever God is or is not, it seems to me that God must be a relational being. In other words, for God to be love, there must be a subject and an object. It's good to remind myself that Jesus emphasized the importance of knowing God experientially—literally to have an intimate connection with God and Christ. Obviously, it's very difficult to have an intimate relationship with an impersonal force. If God is a relational being who desires to know and to be known by those who have been made in God's image, then there must be other beings to direct those affections to.

So, perhaps this, too, is part of the mystery of God. Somehow, in ways we cannot quite comprehend or express, God is a being who is not separate from us, but at the same time is a relational being who loves and receives love from us. Jesus seems to want us to think of God as an "Abba" or a Heavenly Father who is not us but is not separate from us either. This is a paradox, but that doesn't mean it isn't somehow an accurate representation of God's nature.

Let me stop and clarify something here: You don't have to agree with me about any of this. The purpose of this book is not to convince you that your view of God is wrong or that mine is correct. That's not the point. I really do not intend for this book to be persuasive or coercive in any way. I'm just sharing with you where these thoughts have taken me. If anything, I'm just trying to communicate where I am right now and what I'm thinking at this moment in time. In a few years I fully expect to have moved on from this and discovered something new or changed my mind about a few things.

The reason I'm writing this book is partly to put everything down on the page so I can understand all of it better. Because, as I've said before, I process things verbally and writing things down like this—as a writer—really helps me to get my ideas out of my head and on to the page where I can look at them, ponder them, and stir in another layer of ideas as I go.

So, I guess what I'm saying is that this book is me thinking out loud about God. Please do not feel as if you have to believe what I believe or accept where I'm going at this moment in time.

The truth is, I have never wanted to be anyone's guru and I certainly don't want anyone to believe something simply because I said so. Ultimately, all of us have to follow our own path, and navigate our own spiritual journey. This is mine. I know you have your own. I'm just trying to share the thoughts and ideas that are currently bouncing around inside my own heart and mind. Maybe you can relate, maybe not. Maybe you feel the same way, maybe you don't. Maybe you think I'm on to something, or maybe you think I'm out of my mind. Either way, I hope you'll keep reading because there are some pretty interesting ideas for us to think about in the upcoming chapters.

Are you still with me? I hope so.

Because, as we've seen, there is no real problem with suggesting that Christ was "all and in all" before the foundation of the world, and that Christ filled everything in every way long before Jesus of Nazareth was born. We simply need to rethink what we mean when we say that Jesus became the Christ or that the Christ *became incarnate* in Jesus.

Christian Panentheists would argue that the Christ was manifested in the person of Jesus in a much greater and more profound way than the Christ is [or was] manifested in the rest of humanity or creation. Most have no problem with that idea because they see the Christ as being ever present in all creation at all times but in a more pronounced and more intensely expressed way in the person of Jesus of Nazareth.

So, it would seem that the inner experience of Christ we may have individually is not necessarily the same for everyone, even though the potential to experience Christ is the same for all of us. Some of us may require a bit more awareness to fully realize this potential, and none of us—at least as far as Christian Panentheists are concerned—has ever realized that potential as fully and as completely as Jesus did. Or at least, not as far as we are aware.

With that in mind, let's take one last look at these two different ways of approaching the notion of God.

For a Pantheist—someone who believes that God is the Universe itself—there is no such thing as a God who is separate from or distinct from creation. One could be a Christian Pantheist, for example, and simply say that Christ is in all things and is all things without suggesting that Christ was also a separate being that one could pray to, or relate to, or interact with. The same Christ that was in Jesus is the same Christ that is in me, and in you, and in that tree, or in that flower. Christ is the indwelling Divine presence that permeates all things, everywhere, but Christ is not a person you can talk to or relate to.

For a Panentheist—someone who believes that God indwells the entire Universe—there is no such thing as a person who is not already infused with the Divine Presence of God or Christ. Christ fills everyone and everything in every way and there is nothing in this entire Universe that is not filled with Christ. Yet, we might stop short of suggesting that Christ is the Universe, as if God's existence were expressed solely in the creation. Rather, we would say that God and Christ exist in some sense apart from the Universe, but that they created the Cosmos in order to more fully share God's self with an infinite number of living beings created in God's own Divine image. From this perspective, we are not God the same way God is God, but we are filled with the fullness of God. We also cannot exist apart from God, but God can—and does—exist apart from us.

Return to Mystery

To be honest, I think almost all of this discussion may fall under the category of the mystery of God. Because, as we've said before, God is, by definition, a being so far beyond our human capacity to comprehend, that none of us could ever fully understand God in this life. It's the same as trying to explain a four-dimensional universe to a one-dimensional person. You could never fully communicate what a four-dimensional reality is to anyone who existed at a lower dimensional realm.

As much as we cannot help but wonder about these things and try to understand the nature of God in this way, the reality is that it's no different than trying to draw out the concept of "Christ in us" on that napkin. At some point the entire thing breaks down because it's simply not possible to conceptualize a Being so complex and mysterious with our limited imaginations and resources.

As we've already seen, another challenge for us whenever we try to talk about God is the immediate realization that language itself falls woefully short of the task. We just don't have the adequate words or linguistic agility to encapsulate the enormity of God's total existence, or nature, using the tools we currently have available.

God's nature transcends human expression. But, thankfully, what we cannot articulate in words we can certainly experience in silence.

So, perhaps the real problem isn't God's categorization into one theological framework or another. Perhaps the real issue here is that we are somehow still trying to define the undefinable and to understand the incomprehensible.

Even when we acknowledge that we cannot know God with any degree of absolute certainty, we still cannot help but to try to wrap our minds around God and try to relate to a God we can—at least on some level—understand.

But the God you can understand is probably nothing at all like the actual Divine Being that transcends Space and Time.

Now, as hard as it may be, perhaps what we should commit ourselves to is the celebration of the mystery of God and to rest in the reality of the fact that none of us will ever know God intellectually, but that all of us can know God intimately and experientially.

For both Panentheists and Pantheists, it's entirely possible to think of God as being expressed in every individual human being. In other words, one way to relate to or interact with God would be to engage with the God [or the Christ] which is manifest in every individual person.

No matter where we find ourselves leaning in this discussion, I hope we can agree that God is not "up there" or "out there" but "in here." Christ is within each and every one of us. God is with us. God is in us. God is us.

So, if we embrace the notion that God is the One in whom we all live and move and have our being, perhaps it really is true that we are the ones in whom God lives and moves and has God's being?

That's the fascinating mystery of God and humanity, isn't it? Somehow God is manifest in all of us, and all of us are manifested as God.

"I do not think that I will ever reach a stage when I say, 'This is what I believe. Finished.' What I believe is alive...and open to growth."

MADELEINE L'ENGLE

Chapter 10
BEYOND EARTH-CENTRIC THEOLOGY

WHEN NIKOLAUS COPERNICUS FORMULATED his new model of the universe which placed the Sun, rather than the Earth, as the center of our solar system in the 1500's, it quite literally turned science, and theology, upside down.

Perhaps we need another Copernican-level paradigm shift today? What I mean is, maybe we need to move beyond an Earth-centric theology that allows for a more realistic understanding of God and our Universe.

For example, many Christians today still hold on to ideas that whatever God is doing in the Universe it must happen here on this planet to matter. Just the other day I was having a conversation with a friend of mine who said, "Earth can't be destroyed because the Kingdom of God has to come to earth after Jesus makes all things new." But in light of how vast and seemingly endless our Universe turns out to be, the idea that God cannot "bring the Kingdom" or "make all things new" without our little planet seems more than slightly absurd.

Bottom line: Many of the ways we conceive of God, or of ourselves, or of God's ultimate plan for the Universe, are all wrapped up in humanity, and specifically, life on this planet.

Sometimes when people say, "God made man in His image", I have to ask, "I wonder if Dolphins ever think, 'I'm made in the image of God!'" And would a dolphin be wrong to think such a thing? What about a giraffe or an elephant?

This human-centric blind spot we seem to have is also the reason why so many of us bristle at the notion of God being a "She" or insist that God is male, as if God had a penis or a vagina.

We can hardly imagine God without personifying God, and in so doing we make that God a man, or a woman, or at the very least some anthropomorphic being that bears at least some resemblance to ourselves.

I recently watched a fascinating documentary which looked at the cataclysmic disaster that nearly wiped humanity from the face of the Earth at the end of the Ice Age. The subject matter led my wife and I to have a conversation about how fragile life on this planet truly is and how there are a variety of similar disasters that could easily erase all human life [or at least most of it] in a matter of hours or days.

For example, a single solar flare could instantly vaporize all life on Earth at literally any moment. Most of us would never know what hit us as the oceans would vaporize and all oxygen would instantly evaporate and every living thing would be charred to a crisp in a matter of seconds.

For the record, solar flares extending beyond the orbit of our planet have been observed in our own lifetime. Thankfully, none of those were pointed towards us. But it could still happen.

Another possible cataclysm might be a planet-killing meteor or comet which strikes the earth with enough force to either throw us out of orbit around our sun, or crack us into pieces, or at minimum create massive tidal waves and unleash catastrophic global earthquakes that wipe out most life on our planet.

Or our existence could be snuffed out by the massive super-volcano sitting just beneath the surface at Yellowstone National Park. Because, one day—and we can't predict when—it will erupt suddenly and throw enough molten ash into our atmosphere to kill nearly all human life on this planet in a matter of weeks.

So, what if one of these events were to happen in our lifetime? Would that mean that God wasn't real? Would it mean God's plans to "make all things new" were thwarted? Would it mean that the Gospel isn't true or that those who follow Jesus [or any other religion] wasted their time?

No, of course not. God is still the One in whom we all live and move and have our being.

If all life on this planet were suddenly wiped out, it would only mean that our time on this planet was over. But there are other planets, and a potentially endless variety of other life forms in this Universe where God—the very same God—is at work, and is being revealed, and is being experienced, and is making all things new.

Death for us here in this reality, on this planet, is not the end of our existence. Our consciousness will always be connected to Christ and if we die here we only awaken again in the heart of the eternal Divine whose existence transcends space and time.

The simple truth is this: What we have is now. What we do right now is all that matters in this life. Who we are now is all that counts in this moment.

Yes, Christ is at work in everything, everywhere, and God is revealed in all Creation. Our life here is meant to be a reflection of the love of Christ for all people and all things.

As long as we continue to hold on to the primitive notion that our planet is where all of God's plans must come to fruition, or that what happens on this planet is the only revelation of Christ in the Universe—or that God's image is merely human—we will miss the bigger picture, literally.

Beyond Humanity

A few years ago when I published my book about the End Times and the Second Coming of Christ—*Jesus Unexpected*—I had some pushback from a few people about how I originally ended things. My conclusion was that everyone would eventually come face-to-face with Christ because we would all die in a few short years, and in that way, we would all live forever in Christ's Kingdom which was beyond space and time.

But a few friends pushed back and asked me to add an Epilogue that gave us some hope for an eventual New Heaven and New Earth here on this planet. So, I thought about it and decided that, sure, why not, I could envision a potential outcome where God's Kingdom plan finally comes to be on this planet and, eventually, at some point in the future, physical humanity comes to embody the reality of Christ's Kingdom here.

Yet, I still can't understand why so many of us insist on the physical fulfillment of such things. As if being alive in the presence of Christ is only "real" if we're all in physical bodies of flesh and bone. I honestly don't understand that.

What is "real" is most likely so far beyond our ability to comprehend or imagine that, in comparison, this physical reality we're in now is most likely about as "real" as a child's crayon drawing hanging on someone's refrigerator.

In other words, things don't have to happen on this tiny speck of a planet, dwarfed by gazillions of other galaxies spread out across an infinite Universe of stars and planets, to be "real" or "true."

This is not to suggest that Christ is not up to something in this reality, or in and through all of us, on this planet, here and now. Honestly, I do believe that we are all part of a Divine plan that is being played out in our midst and that we all have an important role to play. We'll talk more about that later.

But, for now, what I want us to understand is that if Christ is all and is in all, and if we are filled with the fullness of Christ who fills everything in every way, then we need to think a little bigger and expand our definitions of God and widen our expectations of what Christ might be up to in our Universe.

If it all burns up tomorrow, or if you and I breathe our last some unexpected day in the future, all will be well, and all manner of things will be well, and Christ will still be all and in all, forever and ever, amen.

I'm convinced there is still an even more ultimate reality beyond this one. There is a dimension of pure Being just beyond our comprehension.

Who knows? Perhaps, we were formed in our mother's womb in order to be born into yet another womb and eventually, when it's time, we'll all be born yet again into another womb of even greater beauty and wonder into another dimension next door.

Either way, this little planet isn't big enough for what God has in store, and our little body isn't either.

Emerging Consciousness

So, as we grow and mature, we begin to move away from those elementary teachings and we find ourselves letting go of those endless arguments about theology, we are now free to gaze in wide-eyed wonder at the infinite majesty of a Being who transcends knowledge and exceeds our human comprehension.

As we come to rest in the awe of this Divine Being who defies explanation, we start to realize that God is much bigger than our boxes, bigger than our conception of reality, and vastly more expansive than we could ever imagine.

The more we ponder who God is, the more we start to question who we are. If we are beings who are made in the image of this unimaginable entity, then how can we help but reimagine everything?

In our next few chapters I want to stop and consider a few more ideas regarding the illusion of separation between Christ and creation, and between us and everyone else.

I also want us to take some time to really consider the unique identity of Christ and what it means for humanity as a whole.

"It is not the answer that enlightens, but the question."

EUGENE IONESCO

Chapter 11

RAISING OUR CONSCIOUSNESS

NOTHING HAS CAPTURED MY imagination more than the synergy between what Quantum Science has discovered about the illusion of separation and the spiritual reality of Oneness revealed by dozens of mystics across thousands of years of recorded history.

These ideas are embedded in our subconscious. They've been revealed to hundreds of seekers; from shamans and poets to scientists and philosophers, all throughout our existence on this planet. Those who meditate know it. Those who have experienced an altered consciousness know it. Those who have studied the way photons behave at the quantum level know it. Those who are still and silent know it.

We are all connected. There is a unifying force that unites all living things in our universe. It is within you and me and everyone who has ever lived.

Some of us call it God, or Brahma, or the Atman, or the Great Spirit. Others think of it as the Unified Field, or the Quantum Wave, even the Kingdom of God. But no matter what you may call it, we can all see and experience the same truth: God is all and is in all.

This fundamental reality might not be the key to unlocking the mystery of who we are and who or what God is, but it at least may give us a new path to follow and new questions to ask as we navigate this rabbit hole of divine mystery that surrounds us all.

One friend of mine recently asked a very insightful question as we were discussing these ideas. She said, "Was there a time when humanity once knew all of this? Did we forget it? Or lose it? Is it like what happened in the Garden?"

I love that question because I think it helps us stop and consider what some of our myths and metaphors have to show us when it comes to human comprehension and spiritual development.

The story of Adam and Eve in the Garden is a metaphor. I don't believe it actually happened, but I do believe it gives us a way of understanding how and why we sometimes struggle with this simple truth of Oneness and Connection with God and one another.

Here's what I mean: The first people—Adam and Eve—were created in an original innocence where they experienced absolute Oneness with God and each other. Eve was even pulled out of Adam, which suggests that the two of them were once both inhabiting the same body before experiencing that separation process.

The ultimate separation for them came when they ate of the Tree of the Knowledge of Good and Evil. This is a metaphor of duality. Once they eat from it they experience a form of spiritual death where they can only see and reason from a place of good/bad, right/wrong, us/them, etc. This is what shatters their ability to see and experience their original Oneness with God and each other.

This story is the perfect metaphor for our own personal experience as human beings. We are born with an original awareness of our Oneness with God and humanity. But, at some point early on in our development, we begin to observe how the world around us operates on this system of good and evil, right and wrong, us and them; the illusion of separation seeps into our consciousness and we are suddenly cast out from the Garden when we lose that original awareness of connection with all things.

This, I believe, is why Jesus urges us to become like little children again. Because, as he says, "Until [we] change and become like little children, [we] cannot enter the Kingdom of God." [Matthew 18:3]

So, the story serves as a helpful metaphor for how humanity starts out knowing the truth and then slowly falls under the illusion of separation which leads to "death." Jesus comes to lead us into a more abundant life where our eyes are opened and we can truly experience the reality of our Oneness with God and with one another.

It's also a helpful way of understanding how we as individuals need to overcome the illusion of an *us vs them* mentality and become like little children again who have eyes to see the reality that only comes when we embrace the metanoia transformation of our minds.

One of the best tools for expressing this process of awakening is something called *Spiral Dynamics*. Authors Don Edward Beck and Christopher Cowan introduced this theory into the business world in their book, *Spiral Dynamics*, as a helpful tool for classifying organizational leadership approaches. The original concept was developed by psychologist Clare W. Graves who took the Hierarchy of Needs perspective and theorized deeper levels that went beyond mere self-actualization and identified these layers of development we now know as Spiral Dynamics. As he puts it:

> "I am proposing...that the psychology of the mature human being is an unfolding, emergent, oscillating spiraling process marked by progressive subordination of older, lower-order behavior systems to newer, higher-order systems as man's existential problems stage."

Others have taken these ideas and found them to be an exceptionally helpful way of understanding the evolution of human consciousness in general. People like Ken Wilber, for example, in his book *Integral Spirituality*, have found the Spiral Dynamics concept can apply to human spiritual development, as well as to areas of health and wellness.

But, what is it?

In this model there are 8 stages of human consciousness and worldview which are color-coded as follows:

- Beige
- Purple
- Red
- Blue
- Orange
- Green
- Yellow
- Turquoise

Each of these stages has its own unique set of dress codes, communication trends, cultural norms, religious ideology, political structure, art forms, economic models, philosophy, and morality codes.

So, it gets quite deep and layered at times, but for our purposes we just want to look at the higher-level ways of thinking and believing that are expressed in each of these stages.

Here's how they break down according to Spiral Dynamics:

Beige (Me): This is the simplest survival stage. Just do whatever it takes to stay alive. Food, water, shelter and procreation are prioritized over all other concerns. The person, or the society at this level has almost no developed sense of the self. This is the most basic, primitive hunter-gatherer stage of consciousness we can imagine.

Purple (We): As survival becomes less challenging, people begin to move into this next stage where people first began to develop a sense of personhood. One began to realize that they were part of a tribe and that they, personally, had an important identity within that tribe. This is where we start to develop our first sense of community. It's also where we can begin to start wondering about why things happen. For example, why do people get sick and die? Why are the crops being devoured by locusts? The answers to these questions are typically rooted in primitive assumptions about deities who are either angry or upset at us; gods we need to appease to solve these problems that seem outside of our control; things like the weather, or famine, or disease must be controlled by beings who are more powerful than we are. So, this is where our most basic religious beliefs begin to form. Art at this stage usually reflects this tribal identity and how it relates to the spiritual realm.

Red (Us): This is the ego-centric stage where people begin to break away from the simplicity of the tribal identity and start to assert a much stronger "Us vs Them" mentality where anyone who agrees with us is seen as family and anyone who is not us is seen as evil and worthy of death. This is where ideas like slavery, genocide and war really begin to emerge. In this stage no one really takes responsibility for their actions. They tend to blame those "other people" for the violence and cruelty they inflict on them as if they had no other choice. Taking responsibility would be seen as weakness and that is something no one at this stage would ever want to do. This is where Empires begin to form and flourish. It's also where rigid hierarchies developed and classes of people were created where status in the culture was determined by birth, wealth, or some other internal concept.

Blue (Religious): The extreme dehumanization practices that emerged during the Red stage led eventually to the need for a sense of shared humanity. Quite intentionally, rulers of empires recognized a need to introduce and promote religion in order to balance the violent chaos that threatened to undermine society. In Judeo-Christian history, a belief in an all-knowing benevolent deity helped to pull humanity out of the seemingly endless pursuit of violence and war. This led to the Blue stage which was more purposeful and authoritarian. At this stage, people are controlled by religious dogma that establishes the will of God [or gods] and defines right and wrong according to religious texts, commands and rules of conduct that everyone is expected to follow. Failure to obey God's authority is usually followed by torture or death in this world, and an eternal spiritual death or torture in the afterlife. This stage is also where some of the world's greatest atrocities emerge because while people have moved into the Blue stage, they still maintain strong Us vs Them tendencies carried over from the Red stage. The positive consequence of this stage is the emergence of the concept of morality. The negative consequence was religious persecution, martyrdom, and public execution which was mainly driven by an inability to consider perspectives and beliefs other than one's own. This system, based on the concept of absolute truth, was something that took a long time for us to escape. Some of us today are still struggling to find our way out from under this mindset.

Orange (Prosperity): This stage is what largely characterizes the modern world today. People who once thrived at the Blue stage eventually begin to have their doubts about that absolute way of thinking. They start to doubt their place in that system. The Orange stage is all about being free, successful and prosperous. Democracy, free markets, capitalism, science and rationality emerge at this stage. This way of thinking tends to inspire a turn from religion to more atheistic or scientific mindset.

Green (Justice): Our focus on personal success and prosperity in the Orange stage leads us to become more aware of how our success creates suffering for others around us. This is where many social justice movements begin to appear. People come together to share their resources and work together to alleviate economic, social and environmental inequities to improve the quality of life for those who do not have the power, influence or ability to do so themselves. This stage is marked by an extreme distrust for authority and a strong dislike for hierarchy.

Yellow (Collaboration): This stage is where people begin to notice the interconnectedness of everything. Earth is one planet inhabited by one human race which must learn to collaborate together in order to survive and thrive. All of our many diverse cultures, systems, religions, economies and perspectives must be integrated in order for everyone to flourish. This is the first stage of Tier 2. Everyone in all of the previous stages attempts to force their worldview on everyone else because they believe their view is the best. In Tier 2, however, we begin to realize that no one has the absolute correct perspective. We step back and evaluate each of the previous stages to understand why people think and behave in those ways. We can see the progression of humanity from Beige to Green and understand how we got from one to the other without judging those people who are in those stages of human development. Here we begin to become aware of who we are as human beings and understand more of what makes us tick. We are beginning to comprehend human nature without reacting to it with hostility. People at this level often work to help educate people and transform those prior systems to move them along the spectrum into higher forms of thinking.

Turquoise (Christ Consciousness): This is the stage where those in Yellow recognize that, while the problems in our world are caused by the conflicts between the prior stages, the solution to those conflicting worldviews isn't possible without raising the collective consciousness of everyone. This is where we find the mystics, gurus, sages and spiritual shamans in our world. They rarely hold political power or run multi-million-dollar organizations. They do not seek to transform their world from a power-over mindset but from a more humble "power-under" model that awakens individual people one at a time. The wholeness of mind, body and spirit is essential at this stage. An awareness of the Oneness of all things and the rejection of duality and separation between people, nature and the universe is paramount. People at this level have less fear about the future. They trust that everything will work out in the end because there is an underlying and overarching Consciousness that is guiding all life in the Universe. As the mystic, Julian of Norwich wrote, *"All is well, and all will be well, and all manner of things will be well."* Rest, trust, peace, and inner harmony mark the person at this stage of development. People at Turquoise allow the Divine force to flow through them. They experience a genuine connection with everyone, everywhere. They feel a sincere love for all humanity regardless of whether that person loves them or agrees with them. They understand that their life is the same life that permeates all things. They see God in everyone and they refuse to harm or exploit anyone because of that awareness.

As you can see, the highest stage humanity has reached collectively, to this point, is the Green or Justice stage. We really can't point to any nations, cultures or societies today that operate at the Yellow/Collaboration or Turquoise/Christ Consciousness levels. Yes, there are individuals who may have attained this stage of being, but, so far, we have yet to find a way to organize entire cultures around either of these Tier 2 levels.

Personal Dynamics

This spiral development model is helpful on many levels. As individuals we start out, I believe, being born into a state of pure reality where we have no concept of separation or division between us and everything else. But, as we grow and mature physically and cognitively, we begin to take on the shape of the world order that surrounds us. Early on we find ourselves in a world where everything is about ME and our first words are "no" and "mine!" Some call this the "terrible two" stage but it mirrors the Beige level in spiral dynamics perfectly. Eventually we move into the Purple stage of personhood. We start to develop an awareness of who we are in the world. We develop our identity around our first community of family. Then we move into the Red stage around the time we enter school. We have a larger sense of community around our classmates, our teachers, our routine. Then we might start going to church. This is the Blue stage where we develop a sense of God and our new religious ideology begins to shape us accordingly. Once we graduate from high school or college we enter the workforce and discover the Orange stage where financial success defines our actions. Maybe, if we're lucky, we start to develop a sense of compassion for those who find themselves on the margins of our society. This is the Green stage where we start to donate to charities or volunteer at the soup kitchen, or march for equality, or protest injustice. Some of us may make it into the Yellow stage where we step back and realize that everyone and everything is connected to everything else. We see ourselves and God and the Universe as One. This is probably where you're starting to find yourself now, I hope. If so, you're on the right track.

Social Dynamics

We can also chart human development throughout history along the spiral dynamics path. It goes something like this:

Beige: Around 50,000 to 40,000 years ago, humans were focused solely on survival. Things like food, water, warmth, shelter, sex and safety were our only goals.

Purple: Around 40,000 years ago, humans began to form tribes and become hunter-gatherers.

Red: Around the Bronze and Iron Ages, 3,300 BC to 550 BC, civilizations formed and moved into this stage.

Blue: As new moralistic religions such as Zoroastrianism, Judaism and Christianity gained prominence during the Red stage and grew to prominence during Late Antiquity and into the Middle Ages (roughly between the third and seventh centuries) we began to move into the Blue stage. This lasted until the Renaissance which propelled us into the next level.

Orange: An emphasis on science, industry and capitalism and individual achievement took us into what we call the Industrial age.

Green: This stage was relatively recent in our development and was marked by the Hippie Movement of the 60s and culminated in the rise of environmentalism and social justice groups focused on ending hunger, poverty, sexism and racism. Some nations in Europe are moving into this stage by creating new forms of government that address wider concerns at this level but they are not in the majority.

Yellow: We might call this the era of the New Age movement in the West where people began to be "spiritual but not religious" and moved into more Eastern practices of meditation and yoga in hopes of achieving some form of personal spiritual enlightenment. But, so far, humanity has not organized any national governments around this level. It hasn't yet become a wider movement within our human consciousness.

Turquoise: Only a handful of individual figures throughout our history have reached this level. None of us has moved into this stage as a collective society yet, perhaps because we're largely still trying to figure out what the Green stage looks like, and only beginning to consider the Yellow stage.

Of course, it's difficult not to notice how we seem to be moving backwards at this point in time. As more and more people begin to be ruled by Us vs Them thinking and political tribalism fueled by religious identity, we can see how many of us are slipping from Yellow and Green stages back into more primitive, violent and divisive mindsets that we should have abandoned long ago.

Future Dynamics

One may wonder if it's even possible to form a society at Yellow/Collaboration or Turquoise/Christ Consciousness stages since it would essentially require almost everyone alive to operate at one of those higher levels. In other words, as long as there are a majority of people at the Blue/Religious or Red/Prosperity stages, humanity cannot afford to operate at those higher levels of Collaboration or Christ Consciousness. Especially since the violent and hostile worldviews of those lower stages would always threaten to undermine the equilibrium of those at the higher levels.

But, the good news is that we can stand back and look at our progress as a human race from early survival modes to more religious societies and eventually on to stages where collaboration and justice are championed. The truth is, we really have made huge paradigm shifts from extreme selfishness and tribalism to more advanced levels of social awareness and collective action on behalf of the less fortunate. Some of the ways of being and thinking we enjoy today would have been unheard of a few hundred or thousand years ago. The journey may be long and the progress may feel like taking two steps forward and one step back, but the fact is that we've come a long way and we're closer to the top of the spectrum than we've ever been before.

People like Fred Rogers, Julian of Norwich, Mother Teresa, Gandhi, Jesus and Black Elk have shown us that a Turquoise mindset is possible. But, they have also shown us that there is still a danger for those who reach this level. As long as the world around us is at Red or Blue, those in the higher levels may be regarded as a threat and treated accordingly.

As we look at the different levels of consciousness described in Spiral Dynamics we can also see that we, at times, can fluctuate between them depending on the situation. Even if we feel confident that we see and experience reality at the highest level, we can still find ourselves reverting back to tribalism and selfishness at any given moment. Our challenge is to learn how to live at those higher levels of awareness without being pulled back down into the Us vs Them mentality of the world around us.

Will our world ever truly reach this global stage of Christ Consciousness? Who knows? That is the hope. But, if so, it will require a monumental spiritual shift away from individualism and selfishness and a groundswell of spiritual transformation that awakens us to the fundamental Oneness we have with one another, and all things.

In Ken Wilber's book, *Integral Spirituality*, he explains how Christianity in America needs to evolve and change in order to help people continually develop spiritually. In fact, he suggests that it's the inability for Christianity to adapt to these ideas of ascending spirituality that prevents so many of us from maturing beyond the lower tiers.

So, if religion seems to be the main hindrance to human spiritual development in our society, then our religious systems must evolve to help us move away from those early primitive ways of seeing the world. As more and more people inevitably drop out, walk away and leave their narrow-minded religious systems behind, there is still a greater possibility for us to evolve spiritually as a species and embrace more connectedness and Oneness as our guiding principle of being.

Our best hope might be to focus on helping people move into the Yellow stage of Spiral Dynamics. This is the level where everyone can take a step back and notice the way our reality works. From this new perspective, we can start to realize why humanity is the way it is. We can begin to recognize the internal and external forces that have shaped our world. Once we can see clearly what Orange and Red and Blue stages look like, we can shift away from those primitive ways of being and begin to move towards those higher tiers of human development.

We may have to spend a long time in the Yellow stage before everyone is ready to move on to the next levels. Because who's to say that Turquoise is the final stage? Maybe it's just the highest level of consciousness we can see on the horizon? Maybe when or if we begin to operate at this level we'll see even farther ahead at what's to come. That's when our next wave of enlightenment might arrive to whet our appetite for even greater things beyond our imagination.

Ken Wilber and others have theorized a Third Tier of Spiral Dynamics that includes Coral/Indigo, Violet, Ultraviolet and Clear [or Pure] light. But those are mostly hypothetical and largely undeveloped because no one has really seen over the horizon beyond Turquoise at this point.

For now, our attention is better focused on moving into the second tier and helping others to do the same.

But, if humanity is to ever experience anything like the literal coming of the Kingdom of God to earth, it will have to be whenever the majority of us eventually move into the Yellow/Collaborative stage of realization concerning who we are and why we do what we do. Only then can we reach this level of metanoia where humanity can collectively begin to abandon those lower tier ways of being and move forward into the practice of profound connection and oneness found in the Turquoise/Christ Consciousness level.

I believe it's inevitable that more and more individual people will experience this awakening and awareness found in the Collaborative stage. I do have hope that eventually our eyes will be opened and many of us will awaken from our tribalism and the illusion of separation will finally be shattered. Once that happens for the majority of us, there is hope that we can begin to work together across national, religious and ethnic boundaries to join hands and remake our world.

Going back to Jesus, this is what he saw as our fundamental problem. His solution was for us to start over again, to become like little children who are not enchanted with the illusions of division and separation. He prayed that we would be one even as he and the Father were one. He planted the seed in our minds that one day we would awaken to the truth that he is in the Father, and we are in him, and Christ is in all of us. The end of the Spiral Dynamics journey—if it is the end—takes us to the very place that Jesus described: the Turquoise reality that everyone is connected to God and that God is connected to all things.

In my book, *Jesus Unexpected*, I described this as the "slow-motion second coming of Christ" where, one-by-one, Christ is coming alive within each and every one of us until, inevitably, our world is transformed into the image of Christ and the Kingdom of God is fully realized on earth. This is essentially the same as reaching the Yellow/Collaborative and Turquoise/Christ Consciousness tiers of Spiral Dynamics. We're on our way. It's taking a lot longer than we'd like, but we are on the right path. As inevitably as humanity moved from Blue/Religious to Orange/Prosperity, and then to Green/Justice stages, I believe we will eventually find our way into the Collaborative stage, and then, at last, into the stage where our Oneness is finally embraced and humanity returns to that childlike awareness of the Kingdom of God within.

The Christ in us works as us to lead us out of the darkness and into the light. This is what God is up to. This is how the Spirit moves in mysterious ways to lead us into all Truth. This is the slow-motion second coming of Christ and the promised awakening when we all realize that what Jesus and many others told us about is true: Christ is all and is in all. Christ is the one in whom we all live and move and have our being. What we do to one another, we do to Christ, and to ourselves, because we are all in one another. Wars will cease. Poverty will end. Love will consume us. We will be transformed into the glorious likeness of Christ.

I believe that is our destiny. I hold that hope for all humanity. My prayer is that it won't take another two thousand years to unfold.

"Look, and it can't be seen.
Listen, and it can't be heard.
Reach, and it can't be grasped.
Above, it isn't bright.
Below, it isn't dark.
Seamless, unnamable,
it returns to the realm of nothing.
Form that includes all forms,
image without an image,
subtle, beyond all conception.
Approach it and there is no beginning;
follow it and there is no end.
You can't know it, but you can be it,
at ease in your own life.
Just realize where you come from:
this is the essence of wisdom."

LAU TZU, TAO TE CHING, VERSE 14

Chapter 12

PATHWAYS TO CHRIST CONSCIOUSNESS

ARE THERE WAYS TO help speed up this process of moving through the stages of Spiral Dynamics? Can someone in those lower, self-centered or tribalistic stages suddenly find themselves catapulted into the higher tiers of Collaboration or Christ Consciousness? Perhaps. I think it's possible for someone in a middle stage to have an experience that allows them to awaken to the reality of our Oneness with all things as in the Collaboration stage, but it doesn't happen often.

Let's take a look at a few examples of how people can discover those higher realities without having to go through the intervening stages of the spiral.

Near Death Experiences

"As a physician I know that most people don't think about death until they're forced to," says Mary Neal. "But 20 years ago I was not only physically dead, I had been dead for awhile. And that experience radically changed everything about what I am and who I am."

Back in 1999, Mary, an orthopedic surgeon, was in Chile on a kayak expedition with some friends. She was riding a section of the river that was known for its spectacular waterfalls when she accidentally went over a very steep drop and plunged underwater. "I knew it wasn't going to be good," she says. "My boat became pinned, and I was completely submerged under ten feet of water...I could feel my bones breaking. I thought I should be screaming but I wasn't."

That's when Mary died. "I could feel my spirit sort of peeling away from my body, and my spirit was then released up to the heavens."

Mary says that after entering heaven she was greeted by a group of "some-things," admitting she doesn't know what to call them. "People, spirits, beings. I didn't recognize any of them. But they had been important in my life story somehow. Like a grandparent who died before I was born. They were so overjoyed to welcome me and greet me and love me," she says.

Soon she found herself being guided by these beings down a pathway of beautiful flowers. She felt time and space begin to shift. "I experienced all of eternity in every second," Mary says, "and every second expanded into all of eternity."

At the end of the pathway, she came to a large domed structure. "I believe I was in heaven, God's world, whatever you want to call it," she says. "I had an overwhelming sense of being home."

Somehow, Mary could still look behind her and see her body submerged underwater at the waterfall. Her friends were trying to save her, but they couldn't reach her. After nearly 20 minutes they began to wait for her body to float downstream. When it did she was bloated and purple and her eyes were lifeless and fixed. There was no doubt that she was physically dead. After 30 minutes without oxygen, Mary's chances of a physical recovery were statistically at zero.

But, back in the spiritual place where her soul was moving down the path, Mary could see them starting CPR and she could hear them calling her to take a breath. "I did not want to go back down to my body," Mary says. "I had a very, very physical sensation of being held and comforted and reassured that everything was fine."[1]

Surprisingly, the other beings around her told Mary that it wasn't her time yet and that she had to return to her body again because she had more work to do on earth. The next thing she knew she was opening her eyes and looking up at the stunned faces of the men leaning over her body on the riverbank.

Mary, like millions of other people around the world, had just returned from a Near Death Experience. Those who study this phenomenon, like

Dr. Bruce Greyson of the Division of Perceptual Studies at the University of Virginia, believe that there is ample evidence that human consciousness survives beyond the death of the physical body.

What is significant to us is the way these experiences effect the people who die and then return from that place of beauty and light outside of time and space. Many of them report having a renewed sense of peace, and an assurance that we are all connected to God and to one another. They talk about knowing, once and for all, that God is real, and that God is a being of pure love and light. This is one of the ways in which a person might be at a lower stage of the spiral dynamics journey and find themselves catapulted into the higher stages by way of the remarkable experience of dying and coming back again. But it's not the only way.

Psychedelic Experiences

Neal Brennan is a successful comedian who worked as a writer on The Chappelle Show with Dave Chappelle. He has two solo comedy specials on Netflix and he's appeared on dozens of talk shows and performed in some of the most prestigious comedy clubs in the world. But none of that changes the fact that Neal Brennan was overcome by severe depression. He had visited every doctor he could find, taken drugs of many kinds—including Ketamine, a veterinary anesthetic used to tranquilize horses. None of it worked. That's when he tried Ayahuasca.

"I was an atheist," says Brennan, "and then after Ayahuasca journey number three [I said], 'Oh! I'm in the presence of God.' So, I'm just in [God] now; a central creation force that didn't have any rules or laws. I was drowning in incomprehensibility."[2]

"I can't explain it," Brennans says. "It's a feeling. I opened my eyes and I was in the presence of what I can only describe as God and that was the first spiritual experience I had ever had in my entire life. I had 12 years of Catholic school; altar boy, church, mass, and felt nothing. But after that experience it was like, 'Oh, this is what church is supposed to be.' Like the connection to the center beam or inner force. It was really profound, and I was no longer an atheist. I now believe in a God."[3]

Brennan's experience is not uncommon. In fact, there are several scientific studies going on right now to try to understand why so many people who take psychedelics—Mushrooms, Ayahuasca, DMT, LSD, Mescaline, Bufo, and Psilocybin—all have very similar "God Experiences" where they encounter a being of pure love and light, become aware of a spiritual plane of reality previously undetected, and enter a new dimension outside of space and time where the connection between all living things becomes abundantly clear.

These are the types of experiences that can transform someone in a lower stage of spiral dynamics into a higher stage like Yellow or Turquoise. Granted, both the NDE and the Psychedelic experiences, which are remarkably similar in nature, may simply be the brain's response to the flood of hallucinogenic drugs—whether naturally produced by the body during a traumatic event, or artificially introduced by taking a controlled substance. But that doesn't mean those experiences are not "real." It may simply mean that some people require these extreme measures to become aware of the higher reality of a Divine presence and the interconnectedness of all things.

"In my experience it's the only way I could have experienced God," says Brennan. "And the good thing is, it's in me now. Because after I was no longer on Ayahuasca I'm still convinced that's as real a thing as has ever happened to me."

In addition to all of this, Brennan says he knew he would never be on antidepressants ever again.

Regardless of how someone comes to realize the Divine Source of the Universe and their Oneness with God and all things, the point is that they do have that realization. Whether through a drug, or meditation, or prayer, or fasting, or holotropic breathing, or a near death experience, the same realization comes and confirms the same reality: *God is all around us and we are all connected to God and to one another*. This realization is what accelerates us on our journey along the spiral path of enlightenment towards a Christlike awareness of the illusion of separation.

Spiritual Experiences

Thankfully, there are many people who don't require psychedelic drugs or near-death experiences to encounter the Divine Source or realize their Oneness with all things. These people are often referred to as mystics, but they may be housewives, construction workers, janitors, bus drivers or anyone of us at any time.

Sometimes these mystics describe their sudden awareness of the Eternal Divine as coming after long periods of silence, meditation, prayer or fasting. But sometimes these mystical experiences happen out of the blue without any warning.

Marcus Borg talks about an unexpected shift in his awareness that took place while he was going about his normal routine:

> "For a minute or two (and once for the better part of an hour), what I was seeing looked very different. Light became different—as if there were a radiance shining through everything. The biblical phrase for this is "the glory of God"—as the book of Isaiah puts it, "the earth is filled with the glory—the radiance—of God. The world was transfigured, even as it remained "the same." And I experienced a falling away of the subject-object distinction that marks our ordinary everyday experience—that sense of being a separate self, "in here," while the world is "out there."

> "They were experiences of wonder—not of curiosity, but of what the 20th century Jewish theologian Abraham Heschel called "radical amazement."

"They were also experiences in which I felt that I was seeing more clearly than I ever had before—that what I was experiencing was "the way things are." And they were also experiences of complete peacefulness, marked by a sense that I would love to stay in this mental state forever. Anxiety and distraction utterly disappeared. Everything looked beautiful."[4]

Twentieth-century mystic Caryll Houselander explained her mystical experience in a crowded underground subway car through London that profoundly changed her perspective about the illusion of separation like this:

"I was in an underground train...in which all sorts of people jostled together...quite suddenly I saw with my mind...Christ in them all. But I saw more than that; not only Christ in every one of then, living in them, dying in them, rejoicing in them, sorrowing in them—but because He was in them, and because they were here, the whole world was here, too, here in this underground train; not only the world as it was at that moment, not only all the people in all the countries in the world, but all those people who had lived in the past, and all those yet to come...I came out into the street and walked for a long time in the crowds. It was the same here, on every side, in every passer-by, everywhere—Christ."[5]

Some people experience these sudden shifts in perspective through mystical experiences that transform their understanding of reality on a profound spiritual level. These experiences allow them to move from one lower form of understanding the world to a higher plane that, in terms of spiral dynamics, would qualify as Yellow or Turquoise stages of understanding.

Practical Experiences

Strangely enough, in addition to Near Death Experiences, Psychedelics and profound Mystical experiences, another way to find yourself shifting your perspective into the top levels of the spiral is simply learning about the principles of Spiral Dynamics. In fact, several people have taken courses on this subject, or read books about it, and discovered the ability to step back from themselves long enough to acknowledge the fact that humanity does indeed go through these stages, and once they identify which stage they're currently in, have realized that it makes logical sense to adjust to the higher stages where everyone needs one another and all things are connected.

Others have managed to let go of those self-centered ways of thinking in the lower stages by studying other religions, by becoming a student of world history, or by simply befriending someone outside their own religious or cultural sphere.

No matter how we get there, the point is that it does seem inevitable that humanity will eventually reach those higher stages in the spiral at some point in time. We can track our progress up until now. We can see all the ways we've taken two steps forward and one step back at times, and we can measure the consequences of remaining at those lower stages as compared to the benefits for everyone at the higher stages.

For me, this seems to be evidence that the Christ in all things is responsible for guiding us—patiently, lovingly and inevitably—towards the eventual Christ-consciousness found at the Turquoise stage of the spiral. Perhaps this is the practical way we, as a species, eventually reach the place where The Kingdom of God is among us, and fully realized here on the earth.

It may not come in our lifetime, but I am convinced that one day all of humanity with awaken to the reality of what Christ wanted us to understand all along: *We are not separated from one another. We are all connected to God, and to the rest of creation, in an unbroken quantum expression of the ultimate consciousness which permeates all life in the universe.*

"There is no solution; seek it lovingly."

SOCRATES

Chapter 13

GOD IN ALL OF US

WE'VE COVERED A LOT of ground so far. I hope you've enjoyed the ride. Before we wrap things up, let's take a moment to think about some of the things we've explored.

God is the ultimate consciousness. When Quantum Physicists like the famed Sir James Jean and other scientists make statements to the effect that the universe itself is a great thought or consciousness, it begins to become undeniable that God [or consciousness] is everything, and everything is God [or consciousness].

Perhaps you think that's too far a leap of logic. Maybe it is. But the more I read and study what mystics across a multitude of faiths have to say about consciousness and reality, the more I am becoming convinced that "God/Christ is all and in all" as the Apostle Paul suggests, and that "we are filled with the fullness of [Christ] who fills everything in every way."

The sayings of Jesus from The Gospel of Thomas affirm this. The words of the great Native American mystic and shaman Black Elk do as well. As do the teachings of countless other mystics throughout history.

For example, in the Gospel of Thomas—an early collection of the sayings of Jesus from roughly the same time frame as when the Gospels of our New Testament were written—Jesus says things like this:

> "Jesus said, 'If those who lead you say to you, 'See, the King-
> dom is in the sky,' then the birds of the sky will go before you.
> If they say to you, 'It is in the sea,' then the fish will go before

you. *Rather, the Kingdom is inside of you, and it is outside of you.*" [Saying 3, emphasis mine]

If the Kingdom of God is inside of us, and outside of us, then there is nowhere that God's Kingdom is not, and nowhere we can go to escape this reality of God's eternal presence.

As I continually ponder the identity of Christ and the implications of our own Divine nature, I find myself revisiting the Apostle Paul's encouragement in Philippians chapter 2 where he says:

> "In your relationships with one another, *have the same mind-set as Christ Jesus: Who, being in very nature God,* did not consider equality with God something to be used to his own advantage; rather, he made himself nothing by taking the very nature of a servant, being made in human likeness." [v. 5-7; emphasis mine]

What I noticed was the statement at the very beginning of the section where Paul says that we should have the "same mindset as Christ Jesus, who, being in very nature God..." and it struck me much differently than before: *"We should have the same mindset as Jesus who was, [like us], in very nature God."*

Now, I understand that what's being said in this passage is more about how we interact in our "relationships with one another" as Paul uses the analogy of how Jesus reacted when he knew he was "in very nature God" and that our reaction should be the same as his reaction: to become the servant of all.

But, the analogy remains: Our attitude should be the same as Jesus's attitude once he knew he was "in very nature God"; not to "Lord it over" one another, but to accept the realization with humility and serve rather than rule; to give rather than demand; to share rather than grasp.

Why? Because we realize that our Divinity is what unites us all as one. Because *God is in all of us, and, just maybe, God is all of us.*

I don't mean this in the Pantheistic way we've previously explored. I mean this in the sense that the Divine Mystery of God is in everyone, and, collectively, in some strange, unimaginable way, God is also living and moving and having God's being as all of us.

Remember when we discussed the way Jesus was called a heretic and threatened with charges of blasphemy for saying "Before Abraham was, I Am," in the Gospel of John, and how his response to those who took issue with his claim of shared Divinity with the Father was simply that the Scriptures affirmed that we are, indeed, gods. In other words: Our own scriptures confirm that God has called us gods, so why does it surprise us when we hear someone say this? As we've also already explored, the concept of Deification of humanity was something that almost every major Church Father had no problem taking seriously.

And, as we've also already said, from the Quantum perspective, reality may appear to involve a variety of separate things: trees, cars, animals, elements, etc., but what we're beginning to realize is that this perception is an illusion. The reality is that all of these seemingly disparate things are actually expressions of a single quantum field. There truly is no separation between you and the chair, or between the tree and the sky, or between the ocean and the flame. Everything, everywhere, is the same quantum field manifesting itself in a different form, but in reality it is all still the very same thing.

So, if all fire is the same flame; if all water is the same ocean, if all consciousness is the one consciousness, then maybe it's not too much of a stretch to say that God is, in some sense, all of us.

In fact, perhaps the God we have imagined as separate from Creation and other than us doesn't even exist at all.

Maybe we're not that Supreme Being who sits outside of space and time—because there is no such thing as a God who exists apart from everything—but perhaps it's not too much of a stretch to consider the possibility that God *is* everything—manifested on some level in all of creation—and that, somehow, everything everywhere is therefore an expression of God.

As Richard Rohr explains:

> "Now, 2,000 years ago...this eternal mystery of matter and spirit as one became manifest...in one human person born in Bethlehem, so, as John says, 'so you could look upon it [Christ], so you could touch it, so you could fall in love with it, so you could relate to this Mystery. Because, human beings, we can't love energy. We really can't. We can't fall in love with a force or a concept. The only thing we can really love is [another] person."

> "We found Jesus very lovable...we fall in love with the Incarnation and then, you've got to keep moving! [Because] what's true in Jesus is true everywhere."

Once more let me remind you that the Christ became incarnate in Jesus, but it's not as if this is the first time the Christ filled everything in every way. Christ has always been in all things and all things have *always* been in Christ. So, while it may be true that Jesus was not the first incarnation of Christ, his profound example provides the rest of us with the clearest picture possible of who God is and what God is like; and of who we are, in truth.

So, if God is, in some ways, all of us, then the emergence of the Christ in Jesus points to the reality of the Christ in all of us, and in everything.

But this raises all sorts of other questions, doesn't it? Let's try to take a few minutes here to tackle a few of them.

If God is in all of us, what about sociopaths, psychopaths, murderers, etc.? How can God or Christ be in someone who is capable of such evil?

Great question! Because the idea of Christ in everyone really seems unlikely if you consider all the evil being done in the world. Right? Well, maybe one way to explain this is to say that some people aren't really operating out of their Christ consciousness. Yes, Christ is in them, and everyone else, but some of us are oblivious to the Christ in us and live from the darkness created by this ignorance. Another way to say it might be to suggest that we're all operating at different frequencies or levels of consciousness.

Those who are awakened to the reality of Christ within live out of love and light, while those who are less aware of the Christ within operate out of fear and darkness. The solution to this might be to help everyone awaken to the reality of Christ within them so they can see that Christ is also alive in everyone else around them. Not that we are compelled to do so. I think the Christ consciousness is fully capable of revealing Christ-self within each person without our help. But if we wanted to ease the suffering of those who are unaware of their Oneness with God and with all things, this might be a good way to do that.

We should also keep in mind that mental illness, brain chemistry, addictions, child abuse and other factors may also play a role in these abhorrent behaviors and thereby limit or restrict a person's ability to see or even understand the reality of the Christ within.

So, the fact that some people are compelled to do evil may simply be the lack of an ability to embrace the reality of the Christ within. The solution to this problem of evil and suffering, then, would be to work to help as many people as possible to recognize this reality of the universal Christ who fills them—and everything and everyone—in every way.

If God is in all of us, why is the world so screwed up?

As we said above, the world is screwed up precisely because most of us believe that we are separate from God and that everyone must jump through religious, ethical and moral hoops to achieve or to maintain a connection with God; something everyone already has without trying.

Again, Richard Rohr helps us understand why things are the way they are:

> "When I say 'I believe in Jesus Christ', I'm making two faith affirmations. First, in the person [Jesus], and second in this universe that the person represents. [Jesus] is a stand-in for everybody. He's a stand-in for all things."

> "Because we've failed to make this second affirmation, that's why we've polluted the planet, that's why we have war, that's why we have racism, that's why we've tortured people in the name of the Gospel because we just loved our little private Jesus. We haven't realized that what we do to one we do to everyone. This teaching is hidden in plain sight. You've got to say it before people catch the scandal of it."

> "Jesus says what you do to them you do to me, what you do to me you do to the Father, what you do to the least you've done to me, what you do to your neighbor you do to yourself, and to me. That's called unitive consciousness. That's the knowledge of the Christ. He's looking at reality with the mind of Christ."[1]

If we could help everyone realize they are already one with God and connected to the Divine with an unbreakable chord of love that unites all of us together, many of the world's problems—war, genocide, poverty, hunger, oppression, violence, exploitation, etc.—would eventually evaporate as people began to see Christ in themselves and everyone else around them.

If God is in all of us, what's the point of anything?

For many of us, the daily participation in religious activities is what makes our lives meaningful. We've been told that our religion is the only correct one; our doctrines are the only true beliefs, and so we find meaning and purpose in the practice of our religion.

But, if those religious beliefs are carefully crafted fables to keep us distracted from the reality of our Oneness with God and with one another, and if we can awaken to that reality, then suddenly our sense of purpose and meaning shifts from being religiously correct to simply becoming who we already are.

Our religious leaders have convinced many of us that truth and wisdom and meaning are all "out there" somewhere to be discovered and attained. We've bought into the notion that all of these things—including God—are external to ourselves. So, we spend a lot of our time searching for truth, meaning, wisdom, happiness, and God in books, webinars, conferences, leaders, teachers, religions, etc., never realizing that all of those are internal realities that can only be found by searching within ourselves.

Suddenly we may start to realize that the meaning to life isn't something we need to discover outside ourselves; that it's not some mystery we need to solve or code we need to crack or question we need to answer. Instead, we may begin to suspect that the answer is simply to ask ourselves what makes our lives meaningful. Is it playing with our children, or painting, or gardening, or serving the poor, or caring for animals, or playing music? Whatever it is that gives your life meaning is what you should be doing, and it's different for everyone.

If God is in all of us, what do we do with the Bible, or other world religions like Judaism, Islam, Christianity, Buddhism, Hinduism, etc.?

Once you begin to embrace the idea that God is in all of us, you may find out that your appreciation for other faiths and other perspectives on spirituality gain more significance, not less.

Because rather than believing that there's only one correct religion, and only one right holy book, or prophet, you realize that they all have something profound to contribute to the conversation. Buddhists, Sikhs, Sufis, Jews, Muslims and Hindus all have an element of truth or wisdom for us to consider. We don't take any of them to be the entire story, but we don't dismiss their story simply because it's not our own.

People have been thinking about God for thousands of years now, and none of us has God completely figured out. Listening to each perspective and holding loosely to those stories while gleaning whatever glistens in the light of the mystery of Christ is a worthwhile endeavor.

If God is in all of us, then who am I talking to when I pray?

Who knows? Perhaps you are communicating with God or Christ by the mere act of focusing on God through your thoughts. Perhaps not. There's always a chance you're just talking to yourself, but at the same time, there is the possibility that you are engaged in an endless, infinite dialog within the infinite Mind of Christ that somehow creates a cascade of responses in the spiritual realm that we cannot quite explain.

I used to think of prayer as a direct communication between myself and a personal Being somewhere out there beyond the physical world. I don't think that way anymore. I don't believe that God is far away. I don't believe I need to beg God to do things or that I need to get God's attention.

My views on prayer have shifted a whole lot in the last few years. So much so that I can hardly see any point in blessing a meal before we eat or saying my prayers before I go to bed at night. Yes, I do see great value in expressing gratitude as a spiritual practice, but I don't take the posture that it must be enunciated out loud in the form of a corporate prayer. Being grateful for my life, my family, my friends and the good things that I experience on a daily basis is quite beneficial. Scientific studies have been done on numerous occasions to document the benefits of gratitude and so I regularly take time to practice gratitude in my daily life.

My prayers are more and more sounding like agreements with the Divine presence within that someone needs help, or that some situation requires attention. Often, what I realize is that there is something practical I can do to respond or assist those people who are suffering or hurting. Rather than ask the God "up there" to fix it, I try to collaborate with the God "in here" to be an answer to that prayer in the moment.

Whatever God is, God already knows everything I'm going to say before I say it. God is completely aware of what's going on in my life and in the lives of those I love.

Not only that, God also knows and cares about these concerns more than I do. So, I don't need to inform God of these things, and I don't need to ask God to share my concerns about these problems, and I don't need to beg God to intervene in these situations.

But, at the same time, I'm starting to realize that there may still be some value to agreeing with God about those issues and talking to God about those situations. Not so God will know about those things or care about those problems, but so we can align ourselves together in agreement about everything and attune ourselves to the same frequency of God that resonates around every one of us.

What has helped me in this area has been realizing the fascinating connection between all things that Quantum Physicists call entanglement. Two or more particles can share the same reality and interact across time and space faster than the speed of light. Observation of one particle by another consciousness can change the way that particle behaves, and there appears to be an exchange of information between the observer and the observed that—so far—cannot be explained by scientists.

So, whatever the Christ is, I believe we can say that the Christ is a relational being that responds to observation and attention.

Perhaps prayer is merely an intentional interaction between two or more entities, each of whom is infused with the indwelling presence of Christ. In other words, Christ may be in all things and fill everything in every way, and we may all be filled with God or Christ in one form or another, but at the same time it is the interaction and conversation between discrete elements of the Christ that facilitate action, change and the ongoing transformation of all things.

Honestly, I'm still trying to work all of this out in my own mind. Obviously, I haven't got it all worked out just yet. No one has, and the truth is, no one ever will have it all worked out in this life. But, somehow, I think if God/Christ is in all of us, and perhaps if somehow God is all of us, then maybe there is a fascinating exchange of ideas and a continuous flow of love going on throughout all things in the Universe.

Perhaps it's something like the individual neurons in our brains that continually flash bursts of electricity back and forth to one another, carrying packets of emotion, and insight, synergy and mystery, to-and-fro in an endless, interactive lightning storm of shared communication.

I think the bottom line is this: Keep talking to God in whatever ways make sense to you. Don't worry about getting the formula right. Trust your ability to interact with the Divine presence of Christ which is always as near to you as your very own heartbeat.

If God is in all of us, then are you saying we'll never see Jesus one day in the afterlife or when he returns to make all things new and establish his Kingdom on earth?

This one comes up a lot and in several different places. When I wrote *Jesus Unexpected: Ending the End Times to Become the Second Coming*, people worried that I was saying that Jesus would never come back to earth and we would never live forever in the presence of a literal, physical Jesus.

Honestly, I'm not sure why we must always cling to the physical as "real" and dismiss the spiritual as "imaginary." Perhaps that reaction reveals more about how we tend to think about the differences between spiritual/physical and real/unreal.

At any rate, my response to this so far is to say that I personally don't think we will necessarily see Jesus of Nazareth in the physical realm, or the New Heaven and New Earth reality, which may or may not be on the horizon.

Another reason why I'm not convinced that the idea of a New Heaven and a New Earth is necessarily physical is that, if the Heaven and Earth we experience now is eventually going to pass away, then maybe the point is that whatever reality we awaken into in the next life isn't anything like this Earth or this Heaven but some other, more fantastic reality that makes this one pale in comparison.

This doesn't mean that we won't experience the reality of the presence of Christ in more profound ways than we can possibly imagine once we pass on from this life to whatever awaits us in the next life.

But, I think, for myself, I want to prioritize the importance of realizing that I can and should experience the reality of the presence of Christ right here and right now. Because the reality is that there is nothing separating any of us from Christ in this very moment. We can all experience the reality of God's presence anytime we want. So, there's no need to wait until after we die to enjoy that glorious connection with God.

If God is in all of us, then what is the point of worshipping God?

If we truly embrace the notion that we are in Christ and Christ is in everyone and everything, then we start to realize that relating to God through worship might not make any sense.

In fact, going back to the passage in Philippians where the Apostle Paul urges us to "have the same mind as Christ Jesus, who, being in very nature God…emptied himself and took the form of a servant", etc., we start to notice that, in that same chapter, all of the words we might use to describe what happens when we worship God: surrendering ourselves, humbling ourselves, serving, giving, bowing down, etc. are all the exact same things that Paul says Jesus did towards us.

In other words, we could say that Jesus worships us by surrendering himself to us, humbling himself before us, serving us, giving himself to us, and all the things we usually equate with what happens when we come to worship God.

If our mindset should be the same as Jesus, then the God who worships us seems to be showing us what worship really should look like: not humanity worshipping a God who is high and lifted up somewhere up there in heaven, but a humanity that worships the God who worships us by humbling ourselves to one another and serving one another and giving ourselves to one another the way Jesus did for us.

Our entire understanding of worship, in the modern Christian sense, is rooted in the idea of a God who is separate from us. It involves singing to that God and praising that God in a building while the music plays through the loudspeakers. But that's not the sort of worship Jesus models for us. If we can rethink the whole idea of worship based on observing how Jesus worships us, we might start to understand that God is not separate from us and that the only worship required is to love and serve and honor and bless those other people around us who are made in the same image of God as we are.

Another way of thinking about this is that Jesus seems to have recognized the Christ in all of us and responded accordingly. When we see the Christ in everyone, we will respond by humbling ourselves as Jesus did, and by serving others as he did, and by giving ourselves to others as he did. Because we recognize that Christ is in everyone, we are led to do what Jesus did: to worship the Christ that is everywhere and in everyone.

So, where does all of this leave us now?

As I've gone through the process of putting my thoughts about God down in this book, I've realized something important: God really is a mystery.

I know that. You know that. But once we come to that place of admitting that God is a being so far beyond our comprehension that we can never fully understand God, we can still find ourselves wondering who God is and what God is like. That's sort of what I think I've been processing in this book. Even though I know that God is a mystery, and even though I realize we'll never figure God out, I've still spent a lot of time trying to understand the nature of God in terms I can comprehend. That's why I have continually wrestled with these ideas about whether or not all are in Christ or if Christ is in all, and whether or not this suggests that God is in all things or if God is all things; whether Pantheism or Panentheism is the best way of understanding God or if there's some way to work it all out so that it makes some kind of sense. I even tried drawing out our relationship to God and Christ on a napkin, for goodness' sake.

But, now, finally, I think I know the answer: There is no simple answer. Maybe Panentheism is true in some ways. Maybe Pantheism is true in other ways. Maybe the reality is some mysterious and shadowy region in the overlapping Venn diagram between those two concepts? It's probably even more complex than that, but the point I think I'm slowly coming to realize is that trying to wrap my brain around God; trying to find the answer, working to understand the Divine in my head, is not the way to know God. Because none of us will ever know God by thinking or calculating or conceptualizing. That's just not the way it works.

So, even as we run around in theological circles trying to explain God and understand the incomprehensible, I think it's worth noting that, in some ways, we as human beings cannot help ourselves. We are fascinated by the ultimate mystery in the Universe. We are mesmerized by the unknown. We're all drawn towards the center of reality and the ground of all being. When it comes to God, we're all hopelessly confounded by the unanswered questions inspired by the Divine.

Who is God? Who are we? How does it all work? Where did we come from? Where are we going? How is it all going to work out in the end?

These are the questions we just can't stop asking. These are the mysteries we just can't let go of, and that won't let go of us.

The truth is no one knows the answers to these questions. If they claim to, they're lying, or they're just deceived.

No one knows the answers to those questions because no one can know the answers.

What we have is faith. What we hold is hope.

Our best guesses are really just that.

Is that satisfying? No.

Is that the end of our questioning? Of course not.

Maybe we're all just fated to wrestle with questions that can't be answered and to chew on mysteries that can't be solved.

Maybe that's part of our journey.

Maybe that's part of what it means to be human.

The answers are not to be found in language.

The solutions are not to be mapped out on paper or written down in a book.

Questions are the answer.

Mystery is the reality.

If there is more to be known, it will take more than thinking to unveil.

Our only hope is to become abandoned to the reality of our Oneness with God.

We can't explain it, but we can experience it.

We can't express it, but we can feel it.

We can't describe it, but we can become immersed and transformed by it.

And do you want to know the biggest surprise of all?

God can't stop thinking about us either.

God is fascinated by us.

God's thoughts, night and day, are consumed with each and every one of us.

We are in love with God and God is in love with us.

This is the divine dance of the lover and the beloved.

God is in us and we are in God.

God is the One in whom we all live and move and have our being.

We are the Ones in whom God lives and moves and has God's being.

This is the *Sola Deus*.

END NOTES

CHAPTER 3

1 From *The Experience of God: Being, Consciousness and Bliss*, David Bentley Hart, pg. 43

CHAPTER 4

1 *The Mysterious Universe*, Sir James Jean, p. 137

2 I know that many scholars do not believe that the Apostle Paul wrote Colossians or Ephesians, and I tend to agree. Those were most likely written by some of Paul's own disciples after his death. But, to me, those epistles are still inspired by God and contain what may have been the secret, or private teachings, that he shared with his inner circle.

CHAPTER 6

1 *The Jesus-Driven Life*, Michael Hardin, pg. 276

2 From *Meeting Jesus Again For The First Time* by Marcus Borg, under the section "Wisdom in the Jewish Tradition", pg. 206, Walker Large Print edition.

3 Ibid., pg. 210

4 Ibid., pg. 211

CHAPTER 7

1 From the video Cosmic Christ produced and published by The Work of the People, narrated by Richard Rohr:

https://www.youtube.com/watch?v=IabeHxwSlWU&t=738s.

2 From Unbelievable? Podcast, Is Progressive Christianity a false Gospel?, Randal Rauser and Doug Groothuis:

https://www.youtube.com/clip/Ugkxsr7AyLEeFA5G5HrJ2T5BPRgbITOdBQmS.

CHAPTER 8

1 From a private email correspondence with this author, February 3, 2023.

CHAPTER 9

1 From the video Cosmic Christ produced and published by The Work of the People, narrated by Richard Rohr: https://www.youtube.com/watch?v=IabeHxwSlWU&t=738s.

CHAPTER 12

1 As quoted from the documentary series *Surviving Death*, Episode 1, Netflix, January 6, 2021 and based on the book of the same name by author Leslie Kean.

2 As quoted in the YouTube clip from an episode of PowerfulJRE, *Ayahuasca Made Neal Brennan Believe in God*, from JRE #1898, November, 2022.

3 As quoted in the YouTube clip from the PowerJRE episode, Neal Brennan's Story About Using Ayahuasca for Depression, from JRE #1823, May, 2022.

4 From the article "Mystical Experiences of God" found at www.marcusjborg.org, and previously published in the Washington Post.

5 As told in the book, *A Rocking-Horse Catholic*, by Caryll Houselander.

CHAPTER 13

1 From the video Cosmic Christ produced and published by The Work of the People, narrated by Richard Rohr: https://www.youtube.com/watch?v=IabeHxwSlWU&t=738s.

For more information about Keith Giles,
or to contact her for speaking engagements,
please visit https://www.keithgiles.com/.

Many Voices. One Message.

quoir.com.

Made in United States
North Haven, CT
22 September 2023